AFRICAN AMERICAN HISTORY

THE UNTOLD STORIES

YVETTE LONG

AFRICAN AMERICAN HISTORY

THE UNTOLD STORIES

YVETTE LONG

COPYRIGHT

No part of this publication may be reproduced in any form or by any mechanical means, including storage in a retrieval system or transmitted in any form without permission in writing from the publisher.

Copyright © 2019 Yvette Long

All rights reserved

ISBN: 9781687527806

PREFACE

James Baldwin once wrote, *"The great force of history comes from the fact that we carry it within us, are unconsciously controlled by it in many ways, and history is literally present in all that we do."*

In the 500-plus years since 1513, when the first African-American came to the shores of what is now the United States of America, the focus was on exploration and exploitation, which too quickly turned to a more strictly directed focus on profits, status, and power at any cost or expense. Many of the colonial founders, their families, and descendants did and continue to benefit from this definition of success at the expense of others, mostly African Americans. In the colonial period, it was through slavery; today, it is realized by way of poverty and the business of incarceration, which is an industry generating $3 billion a year.

African-Americans as slaves were stripped of their culture, identity, customs, and even their families and friends. Collectively, this diminished their self-esteem, self-worth, and self-efficacy, leaving them instead with a fabricated identity of themselves, and a notion that they would and could not ever amount to anything other than a slave. In many cases, even the Bible was used as a method to dehumanize them. The slaves, with little knowledge of the language or culture of the whites, were taught and shown falsely documented and fabricated images and accounts of their inferiority and illiteracy as a method of reinforcing and engraining the superiority of whites. This prophecy was not entirely successful due to the strong character traits, mental strength and adaptability of the Africans.

Starting with the trans-Atlantic slave trade, and shifting through time into reconstruction, the Jim Crow laws, segregation, and the systematic destruction of every established black community dating back to before the Revolutionary War, under the direction of wealthy whites, there was and has been a systematic purge of African history and accomplishments. First, blacks were treated as property and not even considered human. Later, some of the blacks were counted as 3/5 of a person, when it suited the purposes of some to do so. A similar white-centric approach was taken to Native Americans and their history. To the victor goes the spoils, and the ability to shape the recording of what happened.

This was not and is not the sentiment or the desire of most Americans, except those who control the purse and minds of those needing to work for a living. Tactics such as hush money, promises of a promotion, along with fear and violence, were and in some cases still are the successful methods used to keep the majority of Americans satisfied, not necessarily happy, in the current system. In its wake, a system thrived on corruption and complacency.

From the passage of the Civil Rights Act to today, there has been an accelerating interest in rethinking and recapturing African-American history, with a focus on accuracy and historical research for finding the truth, for developing a better America. The internet has made this a much easier and possible task.

Fear was not just something experienced by slaves; it was also rampant among the decent and honest whites, who represented the majority of the population. Those Europeans who migrated to this new world did so for a better life, a life where they could experience more freedom and the pursuit of happiness away from a controlling government and class system. Unfortunately, the new world became much like the old they left behind, with the wealthy few controlling the money and therefore the minds of its employees, politicians, and policing systems.

The truth is, if you don't know your history, you lose your civilization and your culture. If the primary history that African-American children are taught boils down to "we came from slaves," we not only lose the rich complexity that is African-American history, but we start children off with a "less than equal" subtlety that disengages them from wanting to learn their history or to be a part of system which stands for principals of justice and equality but yet lives according to a much different system, one of corruption and profits at all cost. This needs to change.

Children black and white are suffering in this current system of too many untruths. Looking at what we know now, we should all seek to establish a nation on the fundamental values of the *Declaration of Independence*: "We hold these Truths to be self-evident, that **all Men are created equal**, that they are endowed by their Creator with certain unalienable Rights that among these are Life, Liberty, **and the Pursuit of Happiness**...."

For these reasons, I decided to create this book: to place a factual and well-researched counter to our common narrative, to capture many of the unwritten stories of African-Americans, and to detail the actuality of African-American history, which is a centuries-long story of challenges, rising to, and overcoming adversity. It's a history to be proud of! There is no reason not to be. Page after page here, you'll find a rich tapestry of African-Americans involved in all aspects of civilization and civilized society, as well as working to improve things both for themselves and for humanity, despite immense and unrelenting opposition, terror, and racism.

Children are our future – and they have a right to a much better future. In order for this nation to heal, those responsible for the inequalities, disparities, and violence must be identified and held accountable for their crimes, so that all of us can exist in peace with the ability to live together under a *truly* equal system of Life, Liberty, and the Pursuit of Happiness. This process starts with an unveiling of the truths and a rebuilding of a just, compassionate, equitable system where all Americans can live together as one united nation and leave behind a better legacy.

As Winston Churchill once said, "**Those who fail to learn from history** are condemned to **repeat it**." But to learn from history, first, you need an accurate, researched rendering of the truth and untold stories. This book provides just that.

SUMMARY

African American History: The Untold Stories, was written to aid young men in America who could benefit from understanding and connecting with their history. An understanding of history helps us to understand who we are while providing direction for who we are capable of becoming. African American History: The Untold Stories was written for African American boys with the interest of providing them insight into a narrative of their forefathers and a more accurate perception of themselves and their potential.

African American History: The Untold Stories is also valuable to educators, individuals who rely upon the events of the past to serve as a guide in preventing repeated past mistakes, and those needing to find the missing gaps to their identity and purpose. The popular and currently told version of American history is missing large segments of the true American History story.

This book connects young African American boys and others to the true history of African Americans here in America. It's the true American History story – untold stories will inspire the reader to achieve to their fullest potential and to work towards a more united, equitable and just America. Our nation has lived in the shameful shadows of the past, in this book the truths are unveiled which will allow us to live more peaceful and harmoniously while demonstrating our greatness in leadership.

CONTENTS

Preface 5

Period 1 - The "Pre-United States" Days (1513-1774) 1

    Juan Garrido Speaks 3

        August 18, 1518 - The Charter From King Charles V Of Spain 5

        The Lands That Would Form The United States Of America 6

        The Earliest European Settlements In The Present-Day United States Of America 7

        Chapter Review 9

    Resilience 11

        Chapter Review 14

    Heroism 15

        Chapter Review 16

    Art 19

        Chapter Review 21

    Literature 23

        Chapter Review 25

    Math And Science 27

        Chapter Review 29

        Additional References … And For A "Deeper Dive" 31

Period 2 - The New Country (1775-1800) 33

    Crispus Attucks Speaks 35

        The American Revolution 37

        Chapter Review 41

    Resilience 43

        Chapter Review 44

    Heroism 47

        Chapter Review 50

    Art 51

        Chapter Review 53

Literature	55
Chapter Review	57
Sports	59
Chapter Review	61
Math And Science	63
Chapter Review	66
Additional References … And For A "Deeper Dive"	67
Period 3 - Antebellum And The Civil War (1801-1865)	**69**
Harriet Tubman Speaks	71
The Expanding Nation	72
Chapter Review	76
Resilience	79
Chapter Review	82
Heroism	85
Chapter Review	88
Art	91
Chapter Review	93
Literature	95
Chapter Review	98
Math And Science	101
Chapter Review	102
Additional References … And For A "Deeper Dive"	103
Period 4 – Reconstruction (1866-1900)	**105**
Abraham Lincoln Speaks	107
Reconstruction Begins	109
Chapter Review	112
Resilience	115
Chapter Review	119
Heroism	121
Chapter Review	126

Art	129
Chapter Review	131
Literature	133
Chapter Review	135
Math And Science	137
Chapter Review	140
Additional References … And For A "Deeper Dive"	142
Period 5 - The Road To Greater Equality (1901-1976)	**143**
Rosa Parks Speaks	145
Summing Up The Decades: 1900s To 1960s	146
Chapter Review	150
Resilience	153
Chapter Review	162
Heroism	165
Chapter Review	171
Art	173
Chapter Review	174
Literature And Music	177
Chapter Review	182
Sports	185
Chapter Review	188
Math And Science	189
Chapter Review	193
Additional References … And For A "Deeper Dive"	195
Period 6 - The Age Of Reckoning (1977-2019)	**197**
A Tv Executive Reflects On 1977	199
Summing Up The Decades, The 1970s To 2010s	201
Cultural Icons	204
Chapter Review	206
Resilience	209

Chapter Review	212
Heroism	215
Chapter Review	218
Art	221
Chapter Review	224
Literature	225
Chapter Review	229
Sports	231
Chapter Review	235
Math And Science	237
Chapter Review	241
Additional References … And For A "Deeper Dive"	243
Appendix 1	245
Appendix 2	253
Reviews	259
Keywords	260

AFRICAN AMERICAN HISTORY

PERIOD 1 - THE "PRE-UNITED STATES" DAYS

1513-1774

Unsigned 16th century engraving of Juan Garrido and Hernán Cortés meeting Aztecs

THE "PRE-UNITED STATES" DAYS, 1513-1774

CHAPTER 1

JUAN GARRIDO SPEAKS

Every history has to start somewhere, and since I was the first free black man to set foot in what is now the United States of America - in 1513, no less - you might as well start with me. My name is Juan Garrido - and I was a free African American, a baptized Catholic, and a Spanish conquistador.

Historians have tried to place my early life in all kinds of places. I was the son of a King. I came from the Congo. I somehow was freed. I bought my freedom. Back and forth they go, and what actually happened isn't really clear centuries later.

But some things are clear from written documents that have been left behind and the work of historians and researchers. Through their efforts, it's clear I worked with Ponce de Leon, who was the Governor of Puerto Rico. When Ponce de Leon left Puerto Rico in early 1513 on a treasure hunt, he took three ships - *Santiago, San Cristobal*, and *Santa Maria de la Consolacion* - and 200 men. I was one of the 200 men on board those ships.

While legend has it, we landed at present-day St. Augustine and were seeking a Fountain of Youth, neither of those things is true. Based on the work of Florida history researcher and nautical expert Douglas T. Peck, our first landing in what is now the present-day United States was proven to likely be further to the south, near present-day Melbourne Beach, Florida - possibly within eyesight of a relatively new Ponce de Leon statue, authorized by the National Park Service in recognition of the accuracy of Peck's research.

On April 2, 1513, Spanish explorer Juan Ponce de Leon set foot on land that is now the state of Florida. In fact, Ponce de Leon named it Florida, or "land of many flowers." He offloaded several people from the ships to take part in a ceremony claiming the land for the King of Spain, and as his right-hand man, I set foot on land and became part of that ceremony.

We didn't stay long. I can't say if it was the mosquitos that made us leave early, but I can tell you that in later years, some soldiers wrote that the mosquitos were so bad in Florida (before "Mosquito Control") that they had to bury themselves in the sand, with only their heads showing, in order to be able to sleep.

By now, you might be saying, "Wow! A free black man was the first to set foot in America!" Some of you might view me as a hero - but there's more to my story, and you may not like all of it.

I was a Spanish conquistador, and that meant I served the King of Spain and did so for over 30 years of my life. I had a pretty long life for the time - born in 1487, died in the 1550s - and did a lot of things. I took part in Spanish attacks on the natives' present-day Mexico City, and became the right-hand man to Hernan Cortez, as the above drawing shows; I am standing next to him on his horse.

As a free man, who set my own course in life, I also captured natives and held several as my personal slaves for years. With their slave labor, I planted the first wheat crop in the Americas. I had a wife and three children and spent my later years on a plot of land granted to me by the King, outside of Mexico City.

Now the idea of the first free black man in America holding Native Americans as slaves (in present-day Mexico) may not make you comfortable. Tough. I was a Spanish conquistador. Gold, land, property, money, good standing with our King - these mattered, a lot. We did everything we did for the glory of Spain and in the name of our King. In 1518, the King of Spain's charter authorized the taking of slaves, starting a process that would impact over 12 million lives after me, across several centuries.

Actually, Native American lives did matter to us conquistadors. We wanted to get as much money as possible for the sale of our slaves, and we wanted them to be healthy, strong, and able to serve us for a long, long, long time.

AFRICAN AMERICAN HISTORY
AUGUST 18, 1518 - THE CHARTER FROM KING CHARLES V OF SPAIN

On August 18, 1518, King Charles V authorized his Flemish courtier Lorenzo de Gorrevod permission to import 4000 African slaves into New Spain, which would eventually include Spanish Florida. Previous Spanish Kings and Queens hesitated to do so - not out of a belief in the dignity and equality of all human beings, but out of concern that native Africans might bring non-Christian religions to the natives in America.

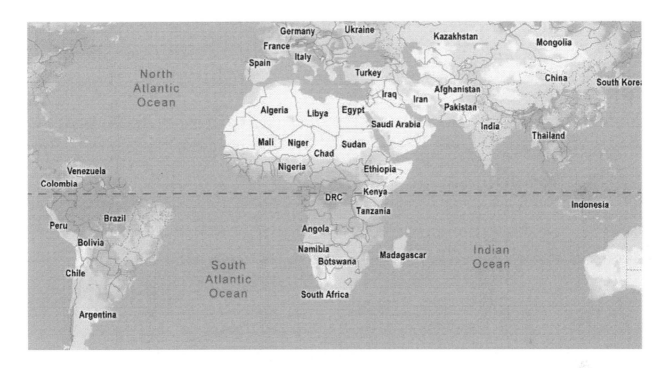

King Charles V figured out a loophole – by baptizing all the African slaves as Christians while they were held on the slave ships. That was the beginning of the trans-Atlantic slave trade from Africa to the Americas - not just the lands that would become the United States of America, but also to the Caribbean, and especially to Brazil.

Most slaves of African origin were taken from the Gold Coast of Western Africa, but there were slaving enterprises set up all over the continent. These human beings were mistreated beyond what many people can imagine today, as they were taken away from their homes and families, could no longer speak their local language or practice their religion, and were forced to work for their entire lives with no compensation. These men and women were sold in the colonies to Europeans, who forced them to work on their land or in their homes for no payment. This form of slavery, which was practiced in the United States, is called "chattel slavery," which meant that human beings were treated like personal property by an owner and thus could be bought and sold. Chattel slaves were slaves since birth. Though these men and women were sold into slavery and taken from their homes, they also practiced resilience, fostered their own culture, and survived in the colonies in several important ways.

THE LANDS THAT WOULD FORM THE UNITED STATES OF AMERICA

Before the United States became a country in 1776, it was a series of colonies, divided between European countries such as Spain, Great Britain, and France. Because Spain was the first country to begin sending missions and settlers to the present-day United States, it established some of the first towns. When the Dutch revolted against Spain and gained their independence, the New Netherlands was formed.

In 1609, the New Netherlands sent English explorer Henry Hudson to find new opportunities, looking for Asia, he stumbled upon territory along the Hudson River. In 1621, the Dutch West India Co. was created and with orders from the King of Holland, the Dutch West India Co. staked out their newly discover, New Netherlands, territory, purchased additional territories and began settling their colony. The main settlement was New Amsterdam, better known today as Manhattan, other territories of the Dutch included New York, New Jersey, Connecticut, Philadelphia and Delaware. There weren't enough colonists to do the work needed.

The Dutch quickly discovered they needed help to develop their new territories. The use of African slaves wasn't a new concept. Europeans were known to have purchased prisoners of war from African kings dating back to the 1400's.

In 1627, the Dutch West India Company brought the first slaves to New Netherland, and they worked to create settlements for the colony. "They cleared land, planted and harvested crops, and built houses, roads, and bridges. They built Fort Amsterdam, cut the road that became Broadway, and fortified a wall along a path that would later be known as Wall Street. Without their work, the colony of New Amsterdam might not have survived."

During the fifty years that the Dutch controlled the New Netherland territories, the legal and social status of the enslaved Africans was not clearly defined, as they followed the same laws as the white population, meaning they could own property, and were granted property for their labor, in addition they enjoyed many of the same civil rights as the whites. The roles of people overall were not so clearly defined, there were whites who weren't really free, many were either indentured servants under contract for several years, apprentices who were bound to a tradesman, and tenants farming land owned by a landlord. It wasn't until when England took the Dutch Colony by force, in 1664, that slavery took a much different path. New Amsterdam was renamed Manhattan, slave trading vessels were soon granted port privileges, and a slave market was established on Wall Street near the East River docks. The lives of slaves became more regulated with laws being passed to control their behavior and status.

Many Europeans had a long standing belief that white Christian men were superior and that it was the natural order of things for them to rule the world. They believed it didn't matter if you were white or black, poor or rich one was born to a particular role and that they held that role for life.

During this time, Great Britain also rivaled Spain, often finding ways to try to best one another and gain more territory. France also battled the two countries, which became particularly important during the French and Indian War (1754-1763). This war was fought between the British and the French through their colonies. This conflict occurred because Great Britain began to infringe on France's colonial holdings. The British won because of the greater population of English colonists and soldiers living in New England, besting the French who had allied themselves with Native American populations, such as the Iroquois.

THE EARLIEST EUROPEAN SETTLEMENTS IN THE PRESENT-DAY UNITED STATES OF AMERICA

In 1521, Ponce de Leon assembled a second voyage, this time to settle a point in Western Florida. Again, he brought several hundred men with him, tools, farm implements, and all the things needed to set up a colony. Unfortunately, he chose a region of Florida populated by the Calusa, one of the most aggressive Native American warrior tribes. The colony didn't last long, what with thousands of poisoned arrows raining down on them, on and off over a period of weeks. One of those arrows killed Ponce de Leon, ending his attempts at colonization.

But you couldn't fault the Spanish for lack of trying. The next settlement attempt was the 1526 voyage of Lucas Vasquez de Ayllon, who landed in present-day South Carolina taking, per researcher Douglas T. Peck, "six ships and around 600 persons, including women, children, and a number of black slaves. There were a few priests in the company but no soldiers, as this was to be a peaceful encounter with friendly Indians who were supposedly ready for conversion to Christianity... (and they also brought) cattle, sheep, pigs, and over 100 horses."

THE "PRE-UNITED STATES" DAYS, 1513-1774

Everything that could go wrong did. The flagship *Capitana* crashed on a sandbar, losing much of its cargo, including some of the food. As the weeks went on, with the prospective settlers "wet, sick, and mosquito bitten," they eventually formed the village of St. Miguel de Gualdape by September 29. Then Ayllon died, and the slaves set fire to the house of his successor and in some cases escaped to hide among the Native Americans - making 1526 the year of the first successful slave rebellion in what is now the United States of America.

There were other early Spanish explorations in the 1500s in what is now the United States, going as far as the lands of Kansas and Tennessee, and as far west as California. Then the French came and tried to secretly put a French settlement called Fort Caroline, Florida into the center of New Spain in 1565. Spanish leader Pedro Menendez de Aviles made sure that didn't last long but realized that Spain really needed a permanent settlement to both successfully claim and defend the land for Spain.

That led to the creation of St. Augustine in 1566, a city on the coast of present-day Florida, and the longest permanent European settlement in the United States of America. Slaves were a significant portion of the community, as the Spanish crown issued licenses to sell up to five hundred slaves. There are theories that Africans arrived with Sir Francis Drake as well in 1586.

Many historians argue incorrectly that 1619 was the first time slaves were brought to America because this was the first time that slaves were brought to the British colonies. The "20 or so African men and women" were brought to Jamestown, Virginia and became a part of the British colonial system. At the time, slavery was not the institution that came to exist in the United States and appears to have been more similar to indentured servitude, where slaves could work and buy their freedom. Later on, in 1662, slavery became a recognized aspect of colonial law.

However, there were many disputes about how to implement slavery. One interesting example is that during the time, in the British colonies, it was considered improper for a Christian to enslave other Christians. Racist legislation followed in the seventeenth century, such as the first anti-miscegenation law, meaning the first law that prohibited racial intermarriage. The period before 1776 offered an opportunity for many enslaved Africans to seek their freedom before the passage of the many laws that took away their freedom.

Meanwhile, before being forcibly taken from the ports along the coasts of African Kingdoms, slaves in Spanish possession were often baptized. In spite of this, many brought their many religions from their homes with them during the long and brutal crossing. Many Africans also worked alongside indentured servants of European birth, who were commonly young men who could not afford life in the new colonies and traded their freedom for income. Indentured servants worked off their debt over the course of several years, exchanging their labor for debt reduction. They were unpaid until their debt was paid off. Some slaves worked in a similar fashion, earning money to eventually buy their freedom.

The culture of this early period was one of greater opportunity for African Americans, as much of the more oppressive structures of slavery had yet to be put in place by the United States Government. This is not to say that life was easy for African Americans but simply to note that buying freedom or converting to Christianity to avoid slavery were more common.

CHAPTER REVIEW

1. Who were the main colonial powers in the United States?
    a. Great Britain
    b. France
    c. Spain
    d. All of the above   *d*

2. How did the enslaved Africans help to build Manhattan, New York City?
    a. They cleared land, planted and harvested the crops that made the colony sustainable
    b. They built and fortified Fort Amsterdam
    c. They cut the road which became Broadway, and fortified the path for Wall Street
    d. All of the above   *d*

3. What is false with how the enslaved Africans were treated by the New Netherlands, a Dutch, Colony?
    a. They were granted their own land to farm
    b. They enjoyed some of the same civil rights as the whites
    c. They were often beaten or hanged if they demonstrated interest in improving their plight in life.   *c*
    d. Their legal and social status was not clearly defined

4. Who fought the French Indian War?
    a. Great Britain versus France and Spain
    b. Spain versus Great Britain and Native Americans
    c. Great Britain versus France and Native Americans   *c*
    d. None of the above

5. What was the first city in the United States where African Americans arrived?
    a. Saint Augustine, Florida
    b. Jamestown, Virginia   *b*
    c. Plymouth, Massachusetts
    d. Port Orange, Florida

THE "PRE-UNITED STATES" DAYS, 1513-1774

6. When were the first Africans most likely brought to the present-day United States?
    a. 1521
    b. 1776
    c. 1619   A
    d. 1565

7. Where were the majority of slaves taken from the continent of Africa?
    a. Gold Coast (primarily Ghana) in Western Africa
    b. Swahili Coast (primarily Zanzibar) in Eastern Africa
    c. Ivory Coast (primarily Cote d'Ivoire) in Western Africa
    d. Cape of Good Hope (primarily South Africa) in Southern Africa

8. Define the core element of "chattel slavery":
    a. Debt bondage wherein a person uses their labor to pay off a loan
    b. Working against one's will due to the threat of violence
    c. Being owned as property, being bought and sold, by another person from birth   C
    d. Being dependent on another person for all one's needs

9. In 1662, slavery became a recognized aspect of colonial law; prior to 1662, black slaves were more akin to indentured servants. Define "indentured servant":
    a. Someone who works without pay for his/her entire life
    b. Someone who works in a prominent household
    c. Someone who works for pay
    d. Someone who works off his/her debt over the course of several years   d

10. What event led to the first slave rebellion?
    a. Explorers going west in search of profitable fur trade opportunities
    b. The Spanish Crown issuing licenses to sell five hundred slaves
    c. African Americans converting to Christianity
    d. Crash of the Flagship "*Capitanna*"   d

11. Many African Americans were which combination of religions during this period?
    a. Catholic and Protestant
    b. Muslim and Catholic
    c. A variety of African religions and Christianity   C
    d. Atheist

CHAPTER 2

RESILIENCE

As aforementioned, the history of this early period before the founding of the United States was one of the potential opportunities for African Americans. As opposed to the structures put in place after 1776, when slavery and racism became more enshrined, this early period was a time of contestation between belief systems and global powers. Many slaves were able to escape the confines of their capture, making new lives for themselves under the protection of a rival colonial power or outside of the law entirely. an interesting trend during this time showing these tensions, Spain and Great Britain held rivaling policies regarding the governance of African Americans in their territories in the present-day United States. Spain formalized a policy in 1693 that offered escaped British slaves a free life and safety from return so long as they converted to Catholicism and served in the Spanish militia. This law was so successful in helping African Americans find refuge that the first free settlement of former slaves was established in Florida, named Santa Teresa de Mosé, near St. Augustine. Fort Mosé is remarkable because it was the first free settlement of African Americans in the United States, under the protection of Jorge Biassou, (1741-1891) one of the first black generals arriving in St. Augustine in 1796, already a legend as one of

the most fiery leaders in the Haitian slave revolt against the French. "The first legally recognized community of ex-slaves was Fort Mose, the northern defense of St. Augustine, founded in 1738 to protect the city from British invasion. In 1740, when General James Oglethorpe attacked from Georgia, it was the Battle of Fort Mose that proved decisive in turning him around and sending him back from where he came. The site of this free black fort is now recognized as a National Historic Landmark and is run by the Florida Park Service. It is considered the focal point for the first Underground Railroad, which ran not from south to north, but rather from the British southern colonies farther south into Spanish Florida, where escaped slaves would be given their freedom", St Augustine Historical Society. A Spanish military base was established near Santa Teresa de Mosé where freedmen could serve. One notable serviceman was Francisco Menendez, who was taken from Gambia and shipped to the Carolinas to work as a slave. He,

along with many others, escaped successfully to Florida and became a captain as the governor noticed his exceptional skill. He contributed to the Free State, by defending St. Augustine from a British attack, and was noticed for his bravery during the battle.

Because of this battle, word spread north to the British holdings of the free life possible for African Americans in Florida. This was one contributing factor to the Stono Rebellion in 1739.

Many newly arrived African Americans revolted, killing their owners, and fleeing from Virginia in order to reach Florida. Although some were killed on the way, many made it to their destination, converting to Catholicism and beginning new lives. The Stono Rebellion remained enshrined in the minds of many settlers, because of their fear that their slaves would also revolt and murder them. Thus, this event was important, because it demonstrated the resistance that many slaves felt to their ongoing unfair circumstances as well as their ability to fight their fates.

These former slaves who made it to Spanish holdings effectively received asylum in Spanish territory, leading free lives and governing their own community. These early communities are remarkable because they show what could have been for the rest of the United States instead of the legacy of slavery. Adding to this, Spain benefited from this law by destabilizing British reliance on the plantation economy in their holdings.

Because of this, not all Africans remained forced into slavery. Some were able to escape in other ways and live outside of the law, such as Nicolas de la Concepcion, who escaped slavery from the coast of New England and became a pirate captain. He used Saint Augustine in Florida as his base and sailed a 140-man crew. He eluded capture for his entire stint as a pirate and most likely lived the rest of his life in Saint Augustine. Historians believe that there were most likely many other escaped slaves and freedmen working on pirate ships. This demonstrates the resilience in many African Americans to escape their bondage and begin a new life and a new trade, challenging the status quo.

Other African Americans made their living outside of the exciting life of piracy. For example, Samuel Fraunces opened the infamous Fraunces Tavern in New York City in 1762 (see image). His tavern played an important role in politics, as it served as a site for General George Washington to gather with his men. This led to Fraunces being chosen to serve as the steward of Washington's home in New York City and Philadelphia. His entrepreneurial spirit showed the many ways that African American men were still able to participate in economic and political life in the years before the founding of the United States.

These outstanding men showcase the other opportunities that African Americans could seize if they were able to escape their bondage. Given their strong sense of self and their ability to find creative means of survival, they demonstrated a strong spirit of resilience in these early years.

THE "PRE-UNITED STATES" DAYS, 1513-1774

CHAPTER REVIEW

1. What profession did some escaped African Americans take up?
    a. Piracy
    b. Innkeeping
    c. Military   *d*
    d. All of the above

2. Which state offered freedom to escaped slaves?
    a. Massachusetts
    b. Virginia   *c*
    c. Florida
    d. Canada

3. Which colonial power offered freedom to escaped slaves and why?
    a. France; to deplete Great Britain's militias
    b. Spain; to destabilize Great Britain's plantation economies   *b*
    c. Spain; to destabilize Great Britain's control over Virginia
    d. Great Britain; to weaken Spanish profits from plantation economies

4. What is the name of the first established free African American settlement in the United States and what year?
    a. Saint Augustine, 1776
    b. Fort Mosé, 1738   *b*
    c. Richmond, 1656
    d. Jamestown, 1693

5. What was the Stono Rebellion of 1739?
    a. When escaped slaves came to Florida
    b. When the British colonists refused to pay British tariffs
    c. When slaves killed their owners and fled to Florida for freedom   *c*
    d. When slaves escaped to become pirates

6. Who did Samuel Fraunces serve after he was welcomed to his inn?
    a. George Washington
    b. Benjamin Franklin   *a*
    c. Thomas Jefferson
    d. Alexander Hamilton

7. Who was known for his bravery while serving in the Spanish militia?
    a. Samuel Fraunces
    b. Nicolas de la Concepcion
    c. Francisco Menendez   *c*
    d. George Washington

CHAPTER 3

HEROISM

There are several examples of African Americans participating in the conflicts that ultimately shaped the United States. One such example is the many slaves who participated in the Seven Years War and the aforementioned French Indian War, fighting on different sides.

African Americans were also leaders during this time of opportunity. One notable example is Jean DuSable's founding of the city of Chicago. DuSable, possibly originating from Haiti or French Canada, settled in the Great Lakes area as a trader and married an indigenous woman. He was known as a handsome and well-educated trader during his lifetime. He is credited with founding Chicago because he established a large settlement that became quite profitable, in what later became the city of Chicago.

Even though the territory was contested by the Spanish, French, and British, DuSable was able to establish his operations in a permanent fashion. He established trading posts that eventually became the city of Chicago, residing in the new city. Yet, the tensions over the new country affected him as well. He showed his loyalty to the new United States when he was arrested by the British military, who suspected him of being sympathetic to the colonial rebellion. DuSable was able to avoid any charges by the British military and continued to support independence.

Seizing opportunities and sacrificing for the political community that would become the United States, the lives of these men are remembered because of their bravery and strong spirits. Although some accounts depict European colonists as the only actors during this period, there are countless African Americans who contributed to the infancy of the United States and ultimately shaped the present-day United States.

CHAPTER REVIEW

1. Who was the founder of Chicago?
    a. Chuck Attucks
    b. Jean DuSable
    c. Francis Drake.
    d. John Bush

2. Who arrested Jean DuSable?
    a. British soldiers
    b. French soldiers
    c. Spanish soldiers
    d. Native American soldiers

3. TRUE OR FALSE: African Americans participated in the many wars that shaped what would become the United States.
    a. True
    b. False

4. Chicago was founded as a:
   a. Port
   b. Series of trading posts   b
   c. Colony
   d. Center of agriculture

THE "PRE-UNITED STATES" DAYS, 1513-1774

CHAPTER 4

ART

Artwork, which can include metalwork, sculpture, woodwork, paintings, sketches, and more, can show the skill of the artist and the materials available at the time. In the colonies of New Spain and New England, many artists produced religious images and sculptures. Landscapes and portraits of colonists are other examples of popular art during this period.

African Americans cultivated their own forms of art and contributed to the developing artistic tradition in the early United States. These forms can be seen in several findings in enslaved communities, such as a small drum, wrought iron figures, dozens of ceramic faces, and more. There are several examples of the New England based engraver Scipio Moorhead and the Baltimore based painter Joshua Johnson producing artwork that would occasionally depict African American subjects. Moorhead's only surviving image was a portrait of the African American poet, Phillis Wheatley (see next section). It is a shame that no other works survived, as Moorhead was described by the *Boston News* as an artist of "extraordinary genius."

Joshua Johnson was the first African American to work full time as a painter, establishing his skill for depicting colonists in portraits. He was born to an enslaved mother but received his freedom early on in life and began advertising his skills as a portrait painter. He primarily made his home in Baltimore but moved frequently to be near his clientele. His portraits included families, which was a rarity during this period of American art, as well as single subjects. His most famous painting, *The Westwood Children,* shows the children of Margaret and John Westwood, who owned a successful stagecoach manufacturing operation (pictured above). This painting hangs in the National Gallery as an example of the skill of this self-taught early African American painter.

Pre-dating Johnson, the earliest evidence of African American art in the U.S. is the work of skilled craftsmen, who were also slaves, from New England. These skilled craftsmen were hired out by slave owners to create items such as instruments, quilts, ironwork, baskets, ceramics, gold work, and more. Some were able to keep a percentage of their earnings and bought their freedom. These craftsmen built many of the most beautiful houses in Louisiana, South Carolina, Georgia, and more. For example, the famous wrought-iron balconies of New Orleans were constructed by slave craftsmen (see above). These craftsmen often were inspired by traditions of arts from their homelands and brought these techniques with them when they were forcibly brought to the Americas. Thus, many of the artistic products of African Americans during this period were inspired by traditions in African art. In this way, their artisanal skills shaped the architecture and craftsmanship of the pre-United States.

There also were African Americans who achieved notoriety due to their artwork. One example of a famous craftsman was John Bush, a soldier fighting on behalf of the British during the French and Indian Wars. He became famous because of the beautiful carvings he would make using gunpowder horns. On the powder horns, he would carve designs and outstanding calligraphy (see above). Because of his efforts, he is considered the founder of American folk art. Some African Americans achieved individual fame for their contributions and artistic pioneering.

These examples show the many ways in which African American men were contributing to the architectural and artistic environment in the area before the country was established. This matters in a broader sense, because of the important role that art played in culture and society overall.

CHAPTER REVIEW

1. What's the importance of studying art during a particular historical time period?
    a. It shows what materials were available.
    b. It shows unique insights into the lives of people during that time.
    c. It shows what was important to people during their lifetime.
    d. All of the above

2. Whose only surviving piece is an engraving of Phillis Wheatley?
    a. John Bush
    b. Joshua Johnson
    c. Scipio Moorhead
    d. Jean DuSable

3. Who is credited as being the first African American to make a living as a painter in the United States?
    a. John Bush
    b. Joshua Johnson
    c. Scipio Moorhead
    d. Jean DuSable

4. What is Joshua Johnson's most famous painting?
    a. *The Westwood Children*
    b. *Portrait of a Family*
    c. *John Westwood*
    d. *Nuestra Senora de los Dolores*

THE "PRE-UNITED STATES" DAYS, 1513-1774

5. What was one thing that made Joshua Johnson's paintings unique?
    a. His portraits of colonists
    b. His depictions of animals
    c. His paintings of chairs
    d. His depictions of families or groups

6. TRUE OR FALSE: Many slaves were able to buy their own freedom by selling the products of their craftsmanship.
    a. True
    b. False

7. What are some of the skills some African American artisans became famous for during this period?
    a. Ironwork
    b. Beading
    c. Needlepoint
    d. Painting

8. Who is considered the founder of American folk art?
    a. John Bush
    b. Joshua Johnson
    c. Scipio Moorhead
    d. Jean DuSable

9. Many African American artisans were inspired by:
    a. Catholic artwork
    b. African artistic traditions
    c. Folk art
    d. British artwork

CHAPTER 5

LITERATURE

As with much artwork during the colonial period, religion was an important and prominent topic for writers. Printing presses from St. Augustine to Boston sent out pamphlets about Puritanism and Catholicism, but the publishing houses of London still held major sway over the literature being produced in the colonies. Early histories, poetry, and religious arguments dominated the new literary tradition in the colonies.

The contributions of African Americans to the literary tradition of the United States also extend to the colonial period, before the country's conception in 1776. When possible, education was a critical component. Some African Americans were able to receive an education in the homes where they worked as slaves, becoming literate and able to participate in the written community of the colonies. The publications of African Americans largely challenged ongoing racist assumptions at the time, showing the intellectual and emotional sameness between human beings.

The oldest known publication of African American literature was produced by Lucy Terry before the United States was even a country. Her piece, titled "Bars Fight," depicted the scene of a terrible massacre in an early colonial time period. Terry was inspired to write the ballad in 1746 after a Native American attack on Deerfield, Massachusetts. As an eyewitness to the attack, she shared the events of the town where she lived as a slave. Her writing has stood the test of time and survived today as an important eye-witness account and work of poetry. Terry was an early example of the unlimited potential and talent that African Americans had. Her work was later used by abolitionists or those who argued for the end of slavery.

Also a woman, Phillis Wheatley published a book of poetry, rendering her one of the most revered poets in the nation. As a child, she was taken as a slave from the Senegal and Gambia region. She was educated and enslaved in a Boston household. Her first poem, "On Messrs Hussey and Coffin," written at the age of thirteen, achieved international acclaim. It was to London that she turned in order to publish her collection of twenty-eight poems. The collection was titled *Poems on Various Subjects, Religious and Moral* and was published in 1773. When she published her works of poetry, she became the most important living example of the intellectual and artistic achievements of African Americans. As a black woman, she broke through the many barriers of racism and sexism at the time to share her artwork with the world. She also used Christianity and morality to invoke a message of equality amongst all people. In this way, Phillis Wheatley joined the tradition of early American poetry and writing.

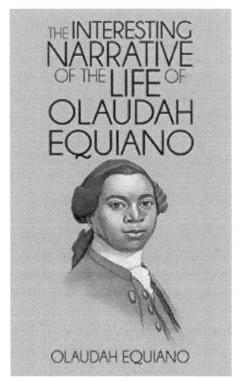

Yet, African Americans also wrote much more than poetry. Olaudah Equiano lived an incredibly fascinating life, which he recounted for his audiences. Although he spent much of his life as a slave, taken from Nigeria when he was a child and sent to South Carolina, he wrote about his life story and successfully published his autobiography. His book, titled *The Interesting Narrative of the Life of Olaudah Equiano* gave a firsthand account of the horrors of slavery. He spent his early years as a slave in the Royal Navy but was eventually sold to a Quaker trader, where he earned his own freedom and became a strong member of the abolitionist movement.

Equiano contributed to the abolitionist movement most directly when he moved to London. He first brought attention to the Igbo cause during litigation for the Zong massacre, which was an atrocity committed by British seamen, who killed over 130 African slaves aboard their ship. Adding to this, Equiano read sections of his work to the Parliament, while they were hearing arguments against slavery. His account was vivid with imagery and extremely well-written, causing his work to spread throughout Europe and the young United States. His work ultimately aided the abolitionist movement around the world, and energized anti-slavery groups and arguments in the early United States, rendering him one of the most important authors of the 18th century.

As this chapter has shown, African Americans contributed to the pre-American literary tradition through poetry, novels, and firsthand accounts. Their writings captivated unique moments in history as well as their own, oftentimes marginalized, experiences. These authors told their own stories, challenged the status quo, and set abolitionist movements into motion, not just in the newly formed United States, but also around the world.

CHAPTER REVIEW

1. Where did many slaves receive an education?
    a. A local school
    b. Their former homes
    c. The home where they forcibly worked
    d. Informally amongst themselves

2. Why were works published by African Americans important in beginning the work of abolition (the end of slavery)?
    a. It allowed them to make arguments for emancipation (being freed from slavery)
    b. It allowed them to show their intellectual capabilities
    c. It allowed them to write about Christianity
    d. It allowed them to document their lives for later abolitionists

THE "PRE-UNITED STATES" DAYS, 1513-1774

3. What is and was the importance of Lucy Terry, the oldest known African American published author?
    a. She was an eye witness to the horrific treatment of African Americans during the 1700's
    b. She is proof of the limitless potential and talent of African Americans
    c. Her work was useful to abolitionist movements
    d. All of the above   *d*

4. What was the name of Lucy Terry's infamous piece?
    a. "Deerfield Massacre"
    b. "1746"   *c*
    c. "Bars Fight"
    d. "The Life and Times of a Slave Girl"

5. Phillis Wheatley was a poet who won national acclaim at the age of thirteen. What year was her collection of 28 poems published?
    a. 1746, Boston
    b. 1778, London   *c*
    c. 1773, London
    d. 1772, Richmond

6. Whose written work depicting unthinkable acts of violence against blacks was used by Parliament in hearings against slavery?
    a. Lucy Terry
    b. Olaudah Equiano   *b*
    c. Phillis Wheatley
    d. John Bush

7. Who was the first African American to write and publish his/her autobiography?
    a. Lucy Terry
    b. Phillis Wheatley
    c. Olaudah Equiano   *c*
    d. John Bush

8. What did Olaudah Equiano contribute to the abolitionist movement?
    a. Firsthand accounts on the horrors of slavery
    b. Religious challenges to slavery   *d*
    c. Legal challenges to slavery
    d. A lawsuit for the Zong massacre

CHAPTER 6

MATH AND SCIENCE

The colonial period in the United States was a time of relative isolation, but a great opportunity, for scientists and inventors. There are many famous examples of founding fathers who also worked as scientists, such as Benjamin Franklin, who conducted experiments that led to greater understandings of electricity, and Thomas Jefferson, who led discoveries in agriculture and geography for the British colonists. Many scientists became attracted to the colonies as a place where they could test their ideas in a freer environment.

Although during this time, there were fewer opportunities for African Americans to become scientists and mathematicians, there are still several notable figures during this period. African Americans were mathematicians, agrarians, scientists, and naturalists, beginning from before the start of the country. Many were self-taught or learned from their parents or took classes in local Quaker schools. The Quakers were a religious community that actively fought slavery and believed in the equality of all human beings. Benjamin Lay (1682 – February 8, 1759) was an Anglo-American Quaker humanitarian and abolitionist. He is best known for his early and strident anti-slavery activities which would culminate in dramatic protests.

One such example of an outstanding African American scientist is Benjamin Banneker, a free African-American almanac author, surveyor, naturalist, and farmer. Born to a former slave father and a free African American mother, Banneker largely taught himself in the fields of astronomy and biology. His grandmother and a Quaker schoolmaster taught him the basics, such as arithmetic, reading, and writing as a child. As he grew older, he began writing almanacs and became extremely successful as an author. His almanacs were so useful because he had an extraordinary understanding of astronomy. Yet, he wrote on many other topics while cultivating his own land, practicing his recommendations. During his lifetime, some of his accomplishments included surveying the original boundaries of the District of Columbia, corresponding with Thomas Jefferson about the Declaration of Independence, and his writings on solar eclipses. Although many of his writings caught fire during his funeral, several of his almanacs remain in use, solidifying his place as one of the most notable early African American scientists. Banneker is an example of one of the most important early African American scientists.

Additionally, Thomas Fuller was also a renowned mathematician during the eighteenth century. Commonly referred to as the "Virginia Calculator," Fuller was taken from the present-day region of Liberia and Benin at the age of fourteen and lived in Virginia. He was never formally taught how to read or write, yet possessed incredible mathematical ability. His skills were used as proof that African Americans were equal to their white counterparts in intelligence. His natural talent and mathematical knowledge astonished everyone who came into contact with him.

These men are examples of the exceptional skills and talent that African Americans held and used during this early period of American history. As agriculture, astronomy, chemistry, and many other fields were just being established, this was a time when many were able to contribute. Some, like Banneker, even used his prominence to advocate for abolition and put pressure on prominent politicians, such as Thomas Jefferson.

By the end of 1774, conditions in the colonies were turbulent, and the discussion of and concerns about revolution were on everyone's mind. Within two years, Thomas Jefferson would make a first stab at declaring the colonies as the United States of America and ending slavery at the same time. His success in declaring independence, and his failure in ending slavery, would set the stage for much of what happened in the United States of America in the 100 years that would follow.

CHAPTER REVIEW

1. Early colonial America was a fruitful place for:
    a. Scientists
    b. Naturalists
    c. Astronomers
    d. All of the above

2. What answer best describes the Quakers?
    a. They were a religious community known to teach blacks to read and write
    b. They were Anglo-Americans who believed in the equality of human beings
    c. They were abolitionists involved in the protest against slavery
    d. All of the above

3. TRUE OR FALSE: Quakers were abolitionists who actively fought for the end of slavery.
    a. True
    b. False

4. Why is Benjamin Banneker remembered?
    a. He could read and write
    b. His writings on abolition (the end of slavery)
    c. His astronomical discoveries and almanacs
    d. His extensive agricultural production and his biological writing

5. With whom did Benjamin Banneker have an infamous correspondence?
    a. Benjamin Franklin
    b. Thomas Jefferson
    c. John Adams
    d. Alexander Hamilton

6. Thomas Fuller was a naturally gifted:
    a. Agrarian
    b. Naturalist
    c. Mathematician
    d. Astronomer

7. Why were Thomas Fuller's skills noteworthy during his time?
    a. It was proof of African American's intelligence
    b. He was never formally taught to read or write
    c. He was like a "Human Calculator" with astounding natural mathematical talent
    d. All of the above

AFRICAN AMERICAN HISTORY
ADDITIONAL REFERENCES ... AND FOR A "DEEPER DIVE"

The Willie Lynch Letter And The Making Of A Slave

By Willie Lynch

Black Indians: A Hidden Heritage

By William Loren Katz

Egalite For All: Toussaint Louverture And The Haitian Revolution

By Noland Walker (Director) Rated: Pg Format: Dvd

Slavery And The Making Of America (Actor, Director)

Rated: PG

Format: Dvd

A Production of Thirteen/WNET

Who Were The Twenty And Odd?

By Kathryn Knight

The Story of The Moors In Spain Paperback

By Stanley Lane-Poole

THE "PRE-UNITED STATES" DAYS, 1513-1774

PERIOD 2 - THE NEW COUNTRY, 1775-1800

THE NEW COUNTRY, 1775 - 1800

CHAPTER 1

CRISPUS ATTUCKS SPEAKS

My name is Crispus Attucks, and I'm – for want of a better phrase - the dead black man in this story.

Now you can take a section out of almost any time period in American history, examine it, and the odds are rather good you'll find a dead black man somewhere in the story. "Tale as old as time," as Disney would say. So what makes me so special? I was the first dead black man at the start of the American Revolution. I even made it into a painting by Paul Revere.

My private life became public when I took a page out of American history and followed in the footsteps of thousands of African-American slaves that came before me: I escaped my captors and ran away, or so said this ad from *The Boston Gazette*, in their October 2, 1750 edition:

Ran away from his master William Brown of Framingham on the 30th of Sept. last a mulatto fellow about 27 years of age, named Crispus, 6 feet and 2 inches high, short curl'd hair, his knees nearer together than common; and had on a light colour'd beaver skin coat, plain new buckskin breeches, blue yarn stockings and a checked woolen shirt. Whoever shall take up said runaway and convey him to his

THE RUNAWAY.

aforesaid master shall have 10 pounds old tenor reward, and all necessary charges paid. And all masters of vessels and others are hereby cautioned against concealing or carrying off said servant on penalty of law.

I like that ad. You don't often get actual details of what an African American wore. You do get those details in escaped slave ads when both who you were and what you wore were considered the slave owner's property.

Like many black men that came before and after me, I was just in the wrong place at the wrong time. Or I felt I was in the right place, doing the right thing when things just went wrong. You weren't there on Monday evening, March 5, 1770. There's no real way to know. Even the artists don't always get it right. Always keep in mind that what we see as history often depends on who is writing it.

But some have to get it right, like those taking notes in a court of law. At the trial of those British soldiers who murdered me in the Boston Massacre, November 27, 1770, they said under oath that the wound that killed me was six inches deep and one inch wide, and killed me instantly.

Centuries later, a PBS documentary about me said I and about 30 others "began taunting the guard at the custom house with snowballs, sticks, and insults. Seven other redcoats came to the lone soldier's rescue, and Attucks was one of five men killed when they opened fire." When John Adams defended the soldiers in the trial, he said I was the leader.

And maybe I was. At 6'2", I always stood out in a crowd, at a time when the average white man was 5'4". Adams said in court that with one hand, I held one soldier's bayonet, while with my other free hand, I knocked another soldier down. He doesn't say which of these two armed soldiers, or the others lined up with them, fired and  promptly killed me at close range. Thanks to John Adams, who later became second President of the United States, history tells us one thing, clearly: each of the five white soldiers on trial was acquitted, of killing me and the others. As I said earlier, "tale as old as time."

I had a background as a seaman, hired by ships on and off for some 20 years before my life ended in Boston, and I was a free man when I was killed.

Each year leading up and into the American Revolution, there was a ceremony to remember me and the others who died that evening in Boston. My name was Crispus Attucks. It sounds pretty close to "Attack Us," which makes it easy for you to remember. Just remember this, too - they didn't just "attack us." Time and again, we African-Americans fought back - and often, triumphed.

THE AMERICAN REVOLUTION

In the way that World War I later set the stage for World War II some 25 years later, the French and Indian War set the stage for the American Revolution. The British mainland put a series of increasing taxes on its British citizens in America, in a series of acts: The Stamp Act, the Intolerable Acts, and more. Colonists complained of impositions, both personal and financial, with little reward for them. These communities began to protest their treatment through boycotts and action, such as the infamous Boston

Tea Party when the colonists threw tea into the sea, challenging the British monarchy. During this time, the colonies became divided between royalists, who maintained their loyalty to the crown, and the patriots, who began to advocate for independence and the establishment of their own country.

There were several sparks that launched the American Revolution - the Boston Massacre, Lexington & Concord - but it was the writing of the *Declaration of Independence* by Thomas Jefferson, and its oral reading in many cities - that declared the colonies as free and independent states, and opened with this provocative idea in the second sentence:

We hold these truths to be self-evident, that all men are created equal, that they are endowed by their Creator with certain unalienable Rights that among these are Life, Liberty, and the pursuit of Happiness.

It was written as "all men" because women were considered property at the time. African Americans often blame Thomas Jefferson for not ending slavery and not ensuring their equality at the time. In actuality, Jefferson did try to end slavery in the *Declaration of Independence*, and wrote this (where "He" below refers to King George III):

He has waged cruel war against human nature itself, violating its most sacred rights of life and liberty in the persons of a distant people who never offended him, captivating & carrying them into slavery in another hemisphere or to incur miserable death in their transportation thither. This piratical warfare, the opprobrium of infidel powers, is the warfare of the Christian King of Great Britain. Determined to keep open a market where Men should be bought & sold, he has prostituted his negative for suppressing every legislative attempt to prohibit or restrain this execrable commerce. And that this assemblage of horrors might want no fact of distinguished die, he is now exciting those very people to rise in arms among us, and to purchase that liberty of which he has deprived them, by murdering the people on whom he has obtruded them: thus paying off former crimes committed again the Liberties of one people, with crimes which he urges them to commit against the lives of another.

Unfortunately, the representatives of all 13 colonies would not agree to the inclusion of this passage in the final version of the *Declaration of Independence*. According to the website blackpast.org, "Decades later, Jefferson blamed the removal of the passage on delegates from South Carolina and Georgia and Northern delegates who represented merchants who were at the time actively involved in the Trans-Atlantic slave trade."

The above passage on ending slavery, which Jefferson wrote for inclusion in the *Declaration*, was omitted and replaced with this (again, where "He" below refers to King George III):

He has excited domestic insurrections amongst us, and has endeavored to bring on the inhabitants of our frontiers, the merciless Indian Savages whose known rule of warfare, is an undistinguished destruction of all ages, sexes and conditions.

The priority was set, and the damage was done. First, the colonies of Great Britain would declare their independence and become the United States of America. Later, at some future point, the issue of slavery would be revisited.

Once the American Revolution broke out, George Washington was appointed to lead the armies of the colonists in fighting the monarchy. A series of early defeats led to great discouragement amongst the colonists, but they quickly recovered and captured several cities, such as present-day Trenton and Princeton, New Jersey.

African Americans, some of whom were freedmen but many of whom were slaves to the colonists, played a significant role in the conflict on both sides. The British army recruited the slaves of colonists, offering freedom in return. In reaction to the shortage of troops, George Washington lifted an ongoing ban on the enlistment of African Americans in the Continental Army and also promised freedom in return. Several all-black units were formed in Rhode Island and Massachusetts. As many as 5000 African American soldiers served the patriot cause during the Revolutionary War. James Armistead, an American spy and double agent, Peter Salem, and others became American patriots and Sons of Liberty. Washington's initial skepticism about permitting African Americans into the ranks of the Continental Army turned to admiration as he saw black men fighting for the same cause he did along with white soldiers. Washington's sentiment towards slavery changed after the war. In 1799, at Mount Vernon where Washington lived and before his death, he arranged for all 123 of the slaves owned by him and Martha to be emancipated after Martha's death, as the slaves were part of their estate and would be handed down to heirs of the estate like other pieces of property. He was the only foundering father to do so.

Peter Salem (1750-1816), an African American man held as a slave from Massachusetts, was one such soldier. During the war, he was freed in order to serve in the militia fighting against the British. He served for five years and became a hero due to his service at the Battle of Bunker Hill. He is credited with fatally shooting the British Major John Pitcairn. His service earned him a shining reputation as he reenlisted each year to serve in the militia until the war was won. After the American Revolution, when he had won his freedom, he settled in Salem, Massachusetts and married, ultimately living a long and satisfying life.

The American Revolution ran from 1775-1783, ending with the United States of America being formally recognized as free and independent of British rule. When the American Revolution was finally won, it took seven years for the central government to get cooperation from states, but the *United States Constitution* was finally ratified in 1788, founding the country and establishing George Washington as the first president.

However, in a second major setback to African Americans after the failure of the Declaration of Independence to ban slavery, the same failure happened in the writing of the *United States Constitution*. Furthermore, Washington reneged on his promise to grant all of the African Americans who served in the war their freedom. Under his governance, many African American soldiers were forced to return to their owners. Even the British, who held New York as their final piece of terrain, disagreed with this and negotiated for the freedom of all the African American men who served with them during the war.

Yes, even back then, there were white people - including very prominent ones - who fought for the equality and freedom of African Americans. Marquis de Lafayette - American war hero, right-hand man to General George Washington, and the guy who helped bring France and major finances in to help win the American Revolution - had this to say, on learning the new U.S. Constitution would not ban slavery: "Had I known, I would never have raised my sword in defense of America."

The American Revolution was over, and the United States of America was formally founded - all setting the stage for what would happen with the still-unresolved issue of slavery.

CHAPTER REVIEW

1. Which states represented in Congress were furious that Jefferson wanted to abolish slavery in the US Constitution and refused to ratify until the anti-slavery statements were removed?
    a. George
    b. South Carolina
    c. Northern delegates who participated in the Slave Trade
    d. All of the above

THE NEW COUNTRY, 1775 - 1800

2. Who promised freedom to the slaves if they fought in the American Revolutionary against Brittan and later reneged?
    a. Thomas Jefferson
    b. King George III
    c. George Washington
    d. None of the above

3. Referring to King George III, who said, "*He has waged cruel war against human nature itself, violating its most sacred rights of life and liberty in the persons of a distant people who never offended him, captivating & carrying them into slavery in another hemisphere or to incur miserable death in their transportation thither.*"
    a. James Armistead
    b. Marquis de Lafayette
    c. Peter Salem
    d. Thomas Jefferson

4. How many African Americans served in the Revolutionary War on the side of the patriots?
    a. 50
    b. 500
    c. 5,000
    d. 50,000

5. Who was the first American president?
    a. George Washington
    b. Thomas Jefferson
    c. The Marquis de Lafayette
    d. John Adams

6. What is known about Peter Salem?
    a. He became a hero due to his service as militia fighting at the Battle of Bunker Hill
    b. He enlisted in the war for five years until the war was won
    c. He won his freedom, married, and lived a long, satisfying life
    d. All of the above

CHAPTER 2

RESILIENCE

The biggest barrier African Americans faced during even this early period of history was their enslavement by white Americans. African Americans found many ways to combat slavery and find freedom and happiness, but it was not always easy. Some fought in the Revolutionary War and were able to gain their freedom only when the British negotiated on their behalf before their departure or they made special appeals to the state legislatures. Others escaped to inaccessible terrains to build community. Others

RICHARD ALLEN

still were able to buy their freedom and the freedom of their families. Rev. Richard Allen 1760 -1831, taught himself to read and later bought his freedom and that of his brother. In 1787, he withdrew from the St. George Methodist Church on account of mean-spirit treatment and restrictions placed on blacks. In 1816, wanting to continue as a Methodist, he called together sixteen representatives from black churches in Maryland, Delaware, and Pennsylvania from which a "church organization" was created. He founded the African Methodist Episcopal (AME) church of America, later becoming the first

African American Bishop of the (AME) church. While many African Americans were forced to continue their lives in slavery, they too built kinships and other networks, fostering their own culture even in the face of terrible oppression.

One interesting example showing the resilience that African Americans faced can be found in North Carolina, where African Americans made up at least 25 percent of the population. Most of the African Americans who lived in this state were enslaved; 5 percent had their freedom. They gave up trying on finding a route to freedom. Many saw the Revolutionary War as an opportunity to free themselves, and some believed that they would be freed for certain if the British won. During this time, in North Carolina and elsewhere, slaves came on the verge of the uprising due to the instability and their desire for freedom. Word spread through the grapevine and plots were hatched to fight for their own freedom. In response, the British began assuring all slaves their freedom if they helped them to win the war. Although they did not win, this period of near insurrection and fighting stood as a testament to the long struggle ahead for African Americans seeking their freedom.

CHAPTER REVIEW

1. What are some examples of African American resilience during this time?
    a. Buying their freedom
    b. Escaping to live in inaccessible areas
    c. Joining the war to gain their freedom
    d. All of the above

2. What percentage of North Carolina were African Americans?
    a. .25
    b. 2.5
    c. 25
    d. 75

3. When the slaves were on the verge of the uprising, to fight for their freedom, how did the British respond?
    a. The waged war again the African Americans
    b. They did nothing
    c. They enlisted them in their army with the promise of freedom
    d. They took away their land

4. Who did most African Americans believe would give them their freedom if they won the war?
   a. The French
   b. The British
   c. The patriots
   d. The loyalists

5. TRUE or FALSE: Rev. Richard Allen founded a "church organization" and the African American Episcopal Church?

   a. True
   b. False

THE NEW COUNTRY, 1775 - 1800

CHAPTER 3

HEROISM

During this tumultuous early period, there were many opportunities for African Americans to become heroes in the newly formed United States. As the country began to determine its own identity and its laws, African Americans played an influential role in these early conversations.

One such example is the life of Lemuel Haynes (1755-1833). His parents were indentured servants, his father African American and his mother white. Lemuel spent most of his childhood as an indentured servant and later a clergyman and a veteran who served during the Revolutionary War. Haynes was the first African American man in the United States to be ordained as a minister. Although Haynes was born in Connecticut but spent his childhood working as an indentured servant in Massachusetts. During this time, he attended church regularly and began to preach his own sermons.

As he matured and when he was finally freed from his indentured servitude, the American Revolution broke out, and Haynes went on to serve during the war in the militia. His most notable military service was when he was a part of recapturing Fort Ticonderoga, where he remained on garrison duty until he became ill with typhus. During his service, he began to write about slavery and the slave trade, preparing sermons and theological works while also criticizing the enslavement of other humans. *He described how the colonists had felt in bondage to Great Britain and longed for freedom in the same way as black communities throughout the newly formed country.* **He wrote, "Liberty is equally as precious to a black man, as it is to a white one, and bondage is equally intolerable to the one as it is to the other."** Upon completing his militia service, he studied theology and became the first African American preacher to receive his preaching license and to preach to a white congregation. His writings and advocacy against slavery became an early foundation combatting the institution. Haynes blazed an important trail for many African Americans to follow.

James Forten (1766 -1842) learned the value of work, at an early age securing his first full-time job at the age of nine years old. He began working on ships at the age of fourteen, traveling twice to Europe before finally settling in Philadelphia in 1790. Here he became an apprentice to sail-maker Robert Bridges, working in a loft where large ship sales were cut and sewn. After the death of Mr. Bridge, Forten purchased the loft. With his keen sense of business and equipment he himself developed, he became one the wealthiest Philadelphians in the city. His business was located on the busy waterfront of the Delaware River, in an area now called Penn's Landing. Forten used his wealth and social standing to work for civil rights for African Americans in both the city and nationwide. He was among the signers of a petition to the U.S. Congress calling for the end of the slave trade and the modification of the Fugitive Slave Law of 1793.

There were also many African American heroes during the fighting of the Revolutionary War. There was Austin Dabney who fought for George, Lambert Latham a member of the Continental Army and over nearly five thousand other African Americans who served with distinction for the American cause from the opening engagements at Lexington and Concord to the climactic siege of Yorktown eight years later, with the help of the 1st Rhode Island Regiment, the British surrendered and the war came to an end.

It was during the winter at Valley Forge that General Washington faced chronic shortages of manpower. Rhode Island general James Varnum proposed a possible solution - he suggested that Rhode Island recruit an all-African American regiment to serve in the Continental Army. The 1st Rhode Island Regiment became known as the "Black Regiment" with 140 of the 220 men consisting of slaves and free black men, producing the first African American military regiment. The 1st Rhode Island Regiment was also one of the first integrated regiment, starting out with segregated units and slowing becoming fully integrated.

Corpus Crispy was the first to die of any race for freedom in the Revolutionary War. James Armistead Lafayette was a spy. The most famous mixed-race fighting unit on the Patriot side was the 1st Rhode Island Regiment.

THE NEW COUNTRY, 1775 - 1800

CHAPTER REVIEW

1. Lemuel Haynes was known for:
    a. Serving as an African American in the Revolutionary militia
    b. Becoming the first African American to receive his preaching license
    c. Preaching to both black and white audiences
    d. All of the above

2. Lemuel Haynes wrote about what staggering comparison:
    a. Religion in Brittan and religion in the newly formed country
    b. Growing up in slavery and growing up in indentured servitude
    c. The bondage experienced by the colonists in Great Britain and blacks in communities throughout the newly formed country.
    d. Living in America and living abroad

3. James Foren is known for:
    a. Being an individual who used his business talents to become one of the wealthiest men in Philadelphia.
    b. Using his wealth and social standing to work for civil rights
    c. Petitioning the U.S. Congress for an end to slavery in 1793
    d. All of the Above

4. James Armistead Lafayette is remembered for:
    a. Becoming the first African American to receive his preaching license
    b. Preaching to both white and black audiences
    c. Serving as a spy during the Revolutionary War
    d. Recapturing Fort Ticonderoga

5. Who was the most famous mixed-race regiment helping to win the battle at Yorktown 1in 1781, which caused the British to surrender and to end the Revolutionary War?
    a. The 24th Massachusetts regiment
    b. The 1st Rhode Island Regiment
    c. The North Carolina Regiment
    d. The 2nd Virginia Regiment

CHAPTER 4

ART

This early period of American art was one of great pride over the founding of the new country. Symbols of patriotism were displayed in the new citizens' homes and on buildings in public spaces, such as the nation's seal, the bald eagle, and famous Americans. The recently acquired freedom also meant that Americans could now engage in international trades, purchasing china from abroad and cabinets from their former homes in Great Britain. This period of artistry was highly indicative of the ongoing cultural context occurring in the newly formed country. African American artists and artisans played an influential role in defining the new country's architectural, aesthetic, and artistic styles.

Although slave art was inherently anonymous - a grave tragedy for art historians today craving more information about their lives - their work influenced every aspect of the newly formed country, from Thomas Jefferson's Monticello furnishings to the mansions of Charleston. These artisans often were heavily influenced by their former homes or their ancestral homes, many times on the West Coast of Africa. Plastic and craft arts dominated these cultures, but still served a function, such as in religious ceremonies or domestic duties. Pottery, basket weaving, making clothing, tools, ivory and bone carving, and more were all demonstrations of this African artistic tradition.

It is also true that slave art forever influenced and shaped the architectural and visual elements of each state. In the Carolinas, skilled slaves produced a wide variety of items that were beautiful as well as useful. African Americans often worked as carpenters, barrel makers, blacksmiths, wheel makers, and many other products.

As aforementioned, there were several African American men who worked successfully as artists during this transitionary period. Scipio Moorhead, Joshua Johnson, and John Bush all made their mark on this period of formative American art. Each contributed a form of painting, sculpture, and carving that serves as an example of mastery during this period. Yet, these men were not the only African American artists during this period. Some African American artists received patronage, meaning financial support for artistic work, by white families who were abolitionists. Artists working in Northern states received better support and were more widely received in society.

Finally, in the record of artwork existing today, there are many portraits and paintings that capture African American experiences during this revolutionary period in the United States. One important example is a portrait of an unidentified Revolutionary War sailor from 1780. Although historians do not know who the artist was, this portrait depicts a common scene as African Americans commonly worked in the navy for both the British and the colonists. Many African American men were already experienced sailors due to their work on merchant vessels or in the British Navy prior to the war. This portrait might be of the most famous black seaman, James Forten. Forten enlisted as a privateer on the Royal Louis but was captured by the British. Once he was freed, he became successful in business and became a leader for the black community in Philadelphia.

As this period in early American art shows, the new country was one that brought the traditions and styles of former homes to the new art scene. The country at the time was also fascinated with forging its own stylistic tradition, with symbols of the revolution and the artistry of African Americans defining this particular early period.

CHAPTER REVIEW

1. What defined this early period of American art?
    a. Images of the Revolutionary War
    b. Nostalgia for Great Britain
    c. Participating in international markets
    d. Patriotism, such as symbols of the new country like the bald eagle and the national seal

2. Where were slaves often taken from that influenced their artwork?
    a. The West Coast of Africa
    b. The East Coast of Africa
    c. The Southern Coasts of Africa
    d. The Northern Coasts of Africa

3. What is one defining feature of many forms of African arts?
    a. Their use of natural materials
    b. The dual purpose as both something beautiful and a tool
    c. The spread of the tradition throughout the continent
    d. Their use of ivory

4. Define "patronage":
    a. A form of indentured servitude
    b. Financial support for artistic work
    c. A form of chattel slavery
    d. Hiring a housekeeper or servant

5. Who was James Forten?
    a. A famous seaman who became a leader in Philadelphia
    b. A famous foot soldiers who became a leader in Boston
    c. A famous spy for the patriots
    d. A famous artist who became a leader in Philadelphia

CHAPTER 5
LITERATURE

Literature in the new country still relied heavily on foreign printing presses, but it began to evolve in a new American style. Several novels were published early on and were well met due to rising literacy rates in the country. Two of the first American novels were Thomas Attwood Digges' *The Adventures of Alonso* and William Hill Brown's *The Power of Sympathy*. There were also several white female authors who participated in the uptick in publications during this time. Susanna Rowson authored *Charlotte: A Tale of Truth*, a romance, in 1971.

During this early period in American history, many African Americans began to use literature to describe the cruelties they had witnessed and borne as slaves. They used the pen to strike up social change and advocate for their communities. One such author was Moses Grandy (1786-unknown). Grandy was enslaved for over forty years before he bought his own freedom by building the Great Dismal Swamp Canal and learning to navigate boats.

His owner cheated him twice when Grandy attempted to buy his freedom, keeping the money and keeping him enslaved. Grandy finally succeeded on his third attempt to buy his freedom, when he was sold to another man.

Grandy experienced many of the horrors of slavery firsthand, which he later translated into his writings. For example, he married a woman whom he wrote that he loved "as I loved my life." After eight months of a happy marriage, she was sold further south. Grandy tried to save her, but there was nothing he could do. He never saw his wife again. This is just one example of the cruelties that Grandy endured. Other examples include being beaten by his owner for not sorting corn husks in the way he saw fit, witnessing the beatings of his fellow African Americans, and enduring the sale of his family members.

Grandy eventually remarried and had several children, whom he was able to free using the money he made navigating ships. Yet, the experiences that Grandy had endured continued to press on him. Because of this, and after he met the abolitionist George Thompson, he began to write an autobiography or a book about his life. His book was named *Narrative of the Life of Moses Grandy, Late Slave in the United States of America*. He also wrote the book to both preserve his experiences in history as well as to raise enough money to buy his other children and family members out of slavery. Yet, his work had tremendous impacts around the world, fueling the abolitionist movement as his firsthand accounts shocked, shamed, and horrified the world.

Similarly to Grandy, John Lea (1773-unknown) wrote an autobiography along with poems about his life before and after his experience as a slave. Lea was born in present-day Nigeria but was sold into slavery in New York City. He taught himself how to read and write and was eventually freed. This enabled him to travel throughout the United States and Europe, eventually working as a preacher. His book, *The Life, History, and Unparalleled Sufferings of John Lea, the African Preacher* is credited with being the first autobiography written by an African American.

Learning how to read and write was the key for us to have these first-person narratives, and to be able to absorb and learn from them today.

CHAPTER REVIEW

1. The publishing industry began to flourish in the United States due to which reason?
    a. The opening of American-based publishing firms
    b. An interest in the new American style of literature
    c. Increasing literacy rates
    d. The inclusion of multiple perspectives in storytelling

2. To what cause did many African Americans dedicate their writings?
    a. Gender equality
    b. Freedom from Great Britain
    c. Education
    d. Abolition

3. For what was Moses Grandy known?
    a. His writings on abolition
    b. His narratives recounting the horrors he had witnessed as a slave
    c. His strength of character and determination
    d. All of the above

4. What horrors of slavery did Grandy endure?
    a. Being beaten
    b. Witnessing the beatings of others
    c. Having his wife sold
    d. All of the above

5. How did Grandy gain his freedom?
    a. He fought in the Revolutionary War
    b. He bought it using savings from his profession
    c. He bought it thrice using savings from his profession and after being sold
    d. He lived in a free territory

6. Define autobiography.
    a. A book written about a person-of-note's life
    b. A novel about abolition
    c. A book recounting one's own life story
    d. A historical work of non-fiction

7. The purpose of *Narrative of the Life of Moses Grandy,* was to do what?
    a. To present a historical account of an African American man's life
    b. To advocate for abolition
    c. To obtain enough money to buy his remaining children and wife from slavery
    d. All of the above

8. For what is John Lea credited?
    a. Writing the first African American autobiography
    b. Preaching in Europe as the first African American
    c. Teaching himself to read and write
    d. Writing poetry

CHAPTER 6

SPORTS

The growth of cities and the increase of wealth in the colonies caused an increase in sports throughout the new country. Games and events occurred commonly during holidays or celebrations, such as Christmas and Easter, and included stoolball, foot races, quoits, and nine pins or bowling. More violent gaming existed too, with the advent of cockfighting, wrestling, and an early version of football. These sporting events were a time to escape the tediousness of daily life and establish stronger ties of community.

For African Americans, those who lived in free states participated in these activities and forms of entertainment. Those who lived as slaves also found forms of recreation to improve their lives and enjoy time spent with one another. This is not to say that life was easy for slaves, as the daily violence, uncertainty, and dehumanization they experienced is unfathomable. Rather, this is to say that African Americans in all situations carried their culture, their communal ties, and their ability to foster recreation with them. In order to participate in sports, slaves would be required to have access to leisure time, which varied depending on the slave owner's particular temperament and rules. Leisure time can be defined as time off from work to relax and participate in activities that one enjoys. For example, an author and journalist named James Buckingham commented, while visiting a plantation, that there were "no games or recreations…provided, nor was there indeed any time to enjoy them if they were." James Williams, a former slave, remarked that "there was little leisure for any of the hands on the plantation. Even on Sundays, there was little or no respite from toil." When a preacher heard that slaves were not even given Sundays off, he confronted the plantation owners, who responded that "if they were not at work, they would be sporting and roving about the fields and woods."

However, this was not the case on all plantations. On some, during holidays where they enjoyed leisure time, slaves enjoyed music as a form of recreation. Many slaves were given Sundays off as well as Good Friday, Christmas Day, and for some plantations, Easter. During these holidays, some slave owners even supplied slaves with food and drinks in order to keep them complacent and happy. These African Americans would enjoy spending times in the woods, gambling, playing music, and dancing for recreation. This ability to have a community, build culture, and joining together showed the resilience of these African Americans during this period.

This historical record from this early period thus gives historians less material to understand how slaves practiced recreation, but it does show that each plantation had a different set of rules. Working within these confines, African Americans fostered their own culture, mirth, and spirit of resilience through music making and games.

AFRICAN AMERICAN HISTORY

CHAPTER REVIEW

1. What are some popular games during this period (1776-1800)?
    a. Foot races
    b. Cockfighting
    c. Bowling
    d. All of the above

2. What sport did African Americans living in the North participate in for fun during this period?
    a. Music
    b. Baseball
    c. The same sports as white Americans
    d. Football

3. Define "leisure time":
    a. Time off from work to relax and participate in activities that one enjoys
    b. Synonymous with holidays
    c. Time to finish one's duties
    d. Time to meet with one's supervisor

4. What did African Americans living in enslavement need to have recreation?
    a. Sundays off from work
    b. Leisure time
    c. A large plantation
    d. An owner with clear rules

5. What days were some slaves given off?
    a. Christmas
    b. Sundays
    c. Easter
    d. All of the above

6. What did many Africans Americans living as slaves enjoy for recreation?
    a. Dancing
    b. Gambling
    c. Music
    d. All of the above

7. What does this period show us about plantations?
    a. That each operated with its own set of rules
    b. That each ran in more or less the same way
    c. That each plantation always gave slaves the day off on Sundays
    d. None of the above

THE NEW COUNTRY, 1775 - 1800

CHAPTER 7

MATH AND SCIENCE

There were many African Americans who possessed the same acumen and skill as their white counterparts in the United States during this time.

As mentioned previously, Benjamin Banneker (1731-1806) was one of the most important contributors to the early scientific history of the United States. This is because Banneker possessed remarkable intelligence and managed to make himself available during times of need. One interesting anecdote tells of a time during the nation's founding when the Frenchman hired by George Washington to design the capital angrily quit, taking all of the designs and plans. Thomas Jefferson requested Banneker be placed on the committee and, Banneker was able to reproduce, from memory alone, all of the architect's plans of streets, parks, and major buildings. He then used his importance to the newly founded capital, and Thomas Jefferson, to challenge Jefferson as the drafter of the Constitution on his hypocrisy with

declaring all men as created equal but continuing to allow slavery. He also included in his letters that it was wrong for Jefferson to own slaves. Among his many achievements as a mathematician, astronomer, agronomist, and surveyor, Banneker is also recognized as making the first functional clock in America.

In 1793, a technological advancement greatly held back the African American fight for freedom: the cotton gin, patented by Eli Whitney, an idea found to be stolen from slaves, thus Eli's patent wasn't renewed, and he did not receive profits. African slaves, because they were not citizens, could not register any invention with the patent office, nor could their slave master or anyone jointly. This made it easy for others to steal their ideas. Referenced by Dorothy Yancy, "Whitney has been charged with borrowing the idea for the cotton gin from a simple comb-like device that slaves used to clean the cotton. Whitney is said to have merely enlarged upon the idea of the comb to create the cotton gin, which works very much like an oversized comb culling the seeds and debris from the cotton."

The cotton gin is a machine that more easily and quickly separated cotton from the seeds of the cotton plant. This allowed for faster and easier processing of cotton into linens and fabrics, while the seeds could be turned into cottonseed oil.

There were also many other important inventions produced by African Americans during and after this important early period. For example, Thomas L. Jennings was the first African American to be granted a patent. He was able to procure this patent for a dry cleaning process he called "dry scouring". Yet Jennings did much more than invent new processes and become the first African American patent holder. He was also a strong abolitionist and worked to support abolition through legal and political organization. He advocated against bans on segregation and fought for African American suffrage, meaning the ability to vote. As such, he was both an important inventor and a contributor to the long fight against slavery.

Jennings was far from being the only abolitionist. As the late 1700s turned forward to the 1800s, slaves began flooding into the United States of America, arriving packed side to side in wooden ships, in voyages that took 3-6 months. According to one source, "Research published in 1794 and referring to how tightly African were packed on shipped, calculated that a man was given a space of 6 feet (length) by 1 foot, 4 inches (width); a woman 5 feet (length) by 1 foot, 4 inches (width); and girls 4 feet, 6 inches (length) by 1 foot (width)."

Dealing with what Lincoln called "the peculiar institution" of slavery, it would grow by the mid-1800s into the dominant issue dividing the new country. The ongoing "question of slavery" needed to be answered - and in the 1800s, it was.

THE NEW COUNTRY, 1775 - 1800

CHAPTER REVIEW

1. What city did Banneker design?
    a. New York City
    b. Boston
    c. Richmond
    d. Washington, DC

2. Who did Banneker challenge on issues of race?
    a. Thomas Jefferson
    b. George Washington
    c. None of the above
    d. All of the above

3. What is a cotton gin?
    a. A machine that collects cotton
    b. A machine that weaves cotton into fabric
    c. A machine that separates the cotton bull from the fibers
    d. None of the above

4. Why was it not clear whether Eli Whitney was the original inventor of the cotton gin?
    a. It was easy to steal ideas from slaves
    b. Slaves couldn't patent their ideas because they weren't considered citizens
    c. Eli Whitney admitted to expanding on an existing idea used by slaves
    d. All of the above

5. Why was the invention of the cotton gin impactful?
    a. It decreased the demand for slave labor
    b. It decreased the demand for fabrics
    c. It increased the demand for cotton made fabrics
    d. It decreased the demand for cotton

6. For what was Thomas L. Jennings known?
    a. Being the first African American inventor
    b. Being the first African American to be granted a patent
    c. Being the first African American to speak with a founding father
    d. Being an abolitionist

AFRICAN AMERICAN HISTORY

ADDITIONAL REFERENCES ... AND FOR A "DEEPER DIVE"

The Narrative of Sojourner Truth

By *Sojourner Truth*

Slavery: Not Forgiven, Never Forgotten – The Most Powerful Slave...

By *Frederick Douglass*

The Half Has Never Been Told: Slavery and the Making of American

By *Edward E. Baptist*

The African Americans: Many Rivers to Cross

By *Gates Jr., Henry Louis* and *Yacovone – available in book, on DVD*

THE NEW COUNTRY, 1775 - 1800

PERIOD 3 - ANTEBELLUM AND THE CIVIL WAR, 1801-1865

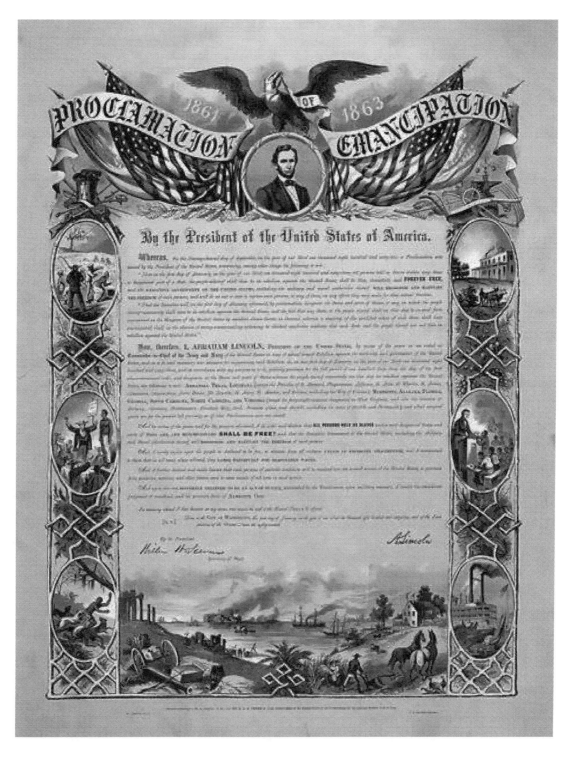

Emancipation Proclamation document

ANTEBELLUM AND THE CIVIL WAR, 1801-1865

CHAPTER 1

HARRIET TUBMAN SPEAKS

My, my, what those Rebel officers must be thinking, seeing me - a 5'2" African American woman - at the front of a Union gunboat here in Maryland. In my dreams, I look at that white plantation house, just want to yell "FIRE!" and watch our cannonballs tear it to bits. But I know it's my people in that house, too - the slaves as servants, the slaves cooking, the slaves cleaning, the slaves taking care of their white children - and I don't want to frighten all those people in the plantation house.

Photo # NH 58767 "The Fight at Corney's Bridge, Bayou Teche, Louisiana ..., January 14, 1863."

HARRIET TUBMAN.

This is one of my many unexpected moments in the Civil War. From the gunboat deck, I look down at the water, and have all these people in front of me, swimming to our boat, carrying chickens in cages over their heads, and baskets of fruit, and whatever belongings they can, looking to our boat as their salvation and freedom. They are in such a panic; the only thing I could think to do was sing to them. So I did, and they calmed down. They knew Harriet Tubman, conductor on the Underground Railroad, and they knew I wasn't going to leave them.

For the Underground Railroad, I made 13 trips to Maryland across 10 years, I rescued 70 slaves, always coming in and out without being captured. The South was so embarrassed they had a huge price on my head. I've been a cook, a nurse, a scout, a spy, and Lordy, now leading a team of three Union gunboats, thanks to the confidence of General Montgomery.

Let's help these poor people get on board now. That's it - come on board. You're free now. You're free. Let me help you with your belongings. Now dry your eyes. You're gonna want to save some of those tears of joy for when you see us burn down that plantation house!

THE EXPANDING NATION

In 1800, the U.S. Congress met in Washington, DC, for the first time. Just a few years later, in 1803, the country finalized the Louisiana Purchase, in which the country doubled in size by adding French territory.

It was not long after that the fairly new country again became embroiled in conflict, declaring war on Great Britain in 1812 due to British interference with the New England Coast. Because of the war against Napoleon in Europe, Great Britain began seizing and blockading the American navy. It did not take long for the two to become entangled yet again in war. Early on, the British gained major ground after defeating Napoleon at the Battle of Waterloo. During this time, they famously burned the White House and embarrassed the country before the world. By 1814, neither side had made major advances and decided to sign a peace treaty.

In this tumultuous time, African Americans again saw an opportunity to continue to advance their cause for freedom and equality. Just as they had in the American Revolution, African Americans enlisted to gain freedom or respect. Free African American men even formed their own unit of freedmen under Andrew Jackson. This unit was imperative in winning the Battle of New Orleans, which occurred after the signing of the 1814 peace treaty. The British went back on their promises of peace and attacked New Orleans, but the American troops, mostly African American and indigenous, held the attacks off, causing the British to suffer two thousand casualties in comparison with their seventy.

Just a few years after the end of the war, in 1819, the Spanish ceded Florida to the United States, causing the country to grow again. This had an enormous impact on the African American communities in Florida who had lived in freedom under Spanish rule. These communities had established free towns and trading posts, integrated into the Creek and Seminole Native American settlements as early as 1771 and served as a safe haven for slaves who escaped during the American Revolution from Georgia and South Carolina. However, as time went on, the territory became a burden for Spanish governing officials to maintain, and granted the territory to the United States through the Adams-Onis Treaty. African Americans who fled to the surrounding Bahaman islands developed new forms of music, dance, and art, as well as their own cultivation of agricultural practices to help their communities thrive.

Following this treaty, Florida became an official state in 1821 and permitted slavery legally. In order to maintain their control over the state, American officials prohibited free African Americans from moving to Florida, sought to expel African Americans from the state, and aimed to force free African Americans back into slavery. This caused an enormous shift in Florida, as wealthy agriculturalists bought up swaths of land to convert into plantations, bringing their own slave labor with them and buying formerly free African Americans. By 1860, nearly half of the population of Florida was enslaved.

The situation in Florida due to the legalization of slavery there demonstrated a tension throughout the rest of the country. In 1820, the Missouri Compromise was made by Congress, which admitted Maine as a free state and Missouri as a slave state into the United States. This limited the number of slave states that could be admitted, in an attempt to limit the scourge of slavery but still appease the wealthy landowners of the South. This argument continued to arise, as it did in 1846 when a representative introduced the Wilmot Proviso, attempting to block and ban slavery in the newly acquired territories with Mexico over Texas. Although the Wilmot Proviso failed, it further intensified the debate about slavery at the national and local levels.

This entire period in the South before the Civil War where there was much debate over the injustice of slavery created a period of unrest and was considered the Antebellum of slavery, which means a particular time period before a war. Antebellum refers to the particular economic boom in the South owing to slave labor. The image of slavery was that everyone in the south owned slaves and profited from this industry. However, a large property owner with hundreds of slave was rare. Three-quarters of Southern whites did not even own slaves; of those who did, only about 10% owned more than 10. The majority of white farmers utilized family labor and were the embodiment of the ideal American: honest, virtuous, hardworking, and independent. The institution of slavery was not part of their everyday life and was not how they prospered. Yet, most non-slaveholding white Southerners identified with and defended the institution of slavery, though many resented the wealth and power of the large slaveholders, they still aspired to join the privileged ranks. Prestige, power, and success were synonymous with the number of slaves you owned. In addition, slavery gave the poor whites a group of people to feel superior to. They may have been poor, but they were not slaves, and they were not black. They gained a sense of power and privilege simply by being white.

The plantation continues to be a symbol of the Antebellum South, as it was the center of economic and cultural means during this time period. This period marked some of the worst atrocities committed against African Americans by white Americans, such as beatings, the sale of family members, sexual assault and abuse, and much more.

When the Civil War broke out in 1861, African Americans had long been ready for their freedom. When Abraham Lincoln was inaugurated as president, secessionist forces attacked Fort Sumter in South Carolina, and seven southern states declared themselves independent from the North. The South became known as the Confederacy, meaning a league or alliance, in this case, of states. The war was fought to end slavery, and the Confederacy sought to separate or secede from the Union, or the North. The war ended in 1865 when General Robert E. Lee surrendered, but the war had been extremely hard-fought and had severely damaged relations in the young country. The death toll reached 625,000, nearly as many American soldiers as having died in all other conflicts put together.

In this conflict to liberate their people, African Americans played a key role for both sides. Over 180,000 African American soldiers served in the Civil War on the Union side alone. Both freedmen and escaped slaves enlisted to contribute to this fight.

Although President Lincoln was concerned that allowing African Americans to enlist would further alienate Border States such as Maryland, by 1862, they needed the manpower, so African Americans were allowed to enlist. These black regiments did not receive equal pay and continued to face discrimination, but continued to play instrumental roles in winning this deadly conflict. These men, the U.S. Colored Troops, comprised roughly 10% of the entire Union Army. African American women also contributed to the war effort, working as nurses, spies, and scouts.

By 1863, Lincoln signed the Emancipation Proclamation, by executive order, which formally and legally freed African Americans and granted them formal citizenship - but only in the states that seceded from the Union.

CHAPTER REVIEW

1. Who was Harriet Tubman?
    a. A spy
    b. A soldier
    c. A leader of the Underground Railroad
    d. All of the above

2. In what year did the newly formed U.S. Congress meet for the first time in Washington, DC?
    a. 1800
    b. 1861
    c. 1776
    d. 1805

AFRICAN AMERICAN HISTORY

3. Why did the 1819 act of the Spanish ceding Florida to the United States have an enormous impact on African Americans?
    a. Africans lived as free men under Spanish rule
    b. African American wanted to go to war with the Spanish
    c. The United States didn't take very good care of its territories
    d. African Americans thought this caused a war with France

4. TRUE or FALSE: Following the treaty of 1821, American legalized slavery in Florida and aimed to force free slaves back into slavery.
    a. True
    b. False

5. What happened to many free African Americans once Florida was incorporated into the United States?
    a. They continued to be free
    b. They were forced to leave and move north to free states
    c. They were forced into slavery
    d. They were forced to leave the country

6. What was the Missouri Compromise?
    a. A compromise that allowed Missouri to be admitted into the union as a slave state in order to satisfy the demands of the wealthy southern.
    b. An agreement that forced free African Americans back into slavery in Florida in exchange for Missouri becoming a free state.
    c. An agreement that allowed Missouri to be admitted to the union as a slave state and Ohio be admitted as a free state
    d. None of the above

7. Define "Antebellum":
    a. A period before a war
    b. The South in the United States before 1861
    c. A period of history during slavery
    d. All of the above

8. How many African Americans served in the Union army?
    a. 180
    b. 1,800
    c. 18,000
    d. 180,000

9. What was the Emancipation Proclamation?
    a. The formal declaration of war between the North and the South
    b. Abraham Lincoln's speech about abolition
    c. The legal document that granted African American slaves freedom and citizenship
    d. The document refuting the Fugitive Slave Act of 1850

10. TRUE or FALSE: Only a ¼ of the whites in the south owned slaves?
    a. True
    b. False

11. TRUE or FALSE: Slavery was an industry dominated by wealthy white landowners?
    a. True
    b. False

CHAPTER 2

RESILIENCE

Following the aforementioned Adams-Onis treaty, Florida became an official state in 1821 and permitted slavery legally. In order to avoid being forced into a life of servitude, free African Americans fled to Cuba, Cape Florida, and the Bahamas. These groups settled primarily on the northwest Andros Island where they established the Red Bays village. They were joined by escaped slaves, most notably by a group of 300 African Americans, who had fled the United States in 1823 using canoes and sloops for their arduous journey.

Under British rule, these islands served as a safe haven for these African Americans, and they passed, by law, that "any slave brought to the Bahamas from outside the British West Indies would be manumitted." Manumitted can be defined as free from slavery. Given this, these islands were a unique space of unique hope and resilience for many Africans and African Americans. For example, in 1834 and 1841, American ships carrying slaves crashed in the British West Indies. In both cases, the slaves on the ships were freed, and Great Britain paid an indemnity to the American government. This gave precedent to the most famous slave revolt in American history.

In 1841, *the Creole* was transporting 135 enslaved African Americans from Virginia to slave markets in Louisiana when 18 of the slaves onboard attacked the crew, killing nearly all and wounding the ship's captain. After discussion on where to set sail, they decided to land in the Bahamas, still under control of the British. All African Americans on board were freed, including Madison Washington, who had already escaped to Canada but was forced back into slavery when he went in search of his wife. Washington, who was said to have instigated the revolt, was detained at first for mutiny. However, upon hearing his argument in court, the Admiralty Court freed Washington and his fellow revolutionaries from any possibility of being returned.

In the United States, California became a fascinating space of opportunity and resilience for African American communities. In 1849, California was declared a free state, writing into the constitution, "neither slavery nor involuntary servitude unless for the punishment of crimes, shall ever be tolerated in this State." The Fugitive Law Act, however, allowed the return of escaped slaves to their owners. Many of the free men came from Northern states like Massachusetts, New York, and Pennsylvania.

In 1848, gold was discovered in the territory, causing a frenzy of movement to the region. Although African Americans were the minority in Gold Rush California, in 1854, a slave, Stephen Spencer Hill, escaped to California to seek freedom and the potential to make it rich when he was brought to California to mine on behalf of his owner, which was a gray area under the law. Hill was later able to purchase farm equipment and avoid being returned to slavery under the Fugitive Slave Act when he pulled out a nine-ounce nugget of gold. Hill is just one example of an African American who used the Gold Rush and the newly defined liberation of California to find freedom.

In the 19th Century, the Sacramento River area developed into an area of many abolitionists. A few blacks had struck it rich in the mines, and others established successful businesses such as hotels, laundries, and restaurants. Some slaves were able to buy their emancipation. "The free black community in Sacramento was strong, organized and relatively wealthy, which led them to finance and support the abolitionist movement and the Underground Railroad in California and throughout the country. The lack of equal civil rights, and often human rights during the 1850s, brought African-Americans together in four Colored Conventions. The sense of community and racial pride instilled by these conventions helped generate California's first black churches, library and the Mirror of the Times, a weekly newspaper that addressed issues for African-Americans".

Throughout the nineteenth century free African American leaders became increasing frustrated with the lack of improvement for African Americans and the enactment of the Fugitive Slave Act. In 1830, the Black National Convention was formalized in Philadelphia to advance their agenda, with the focus being on the abolition of slavery. During the conventions they also advocated for land reform and equal educational opportunities. The Convention was held periodically from 1830-1864.

CHAPTER REVIEW

1. Free African Americans fled where after Florida was incorporated into the United States?
    a. Cuba
    b. The Bahamas
    c. Outer islands of Florida
    d. All of the above

2. Which island became particularly prominent as a free settlement for African Americans fleeing from slavery in Florida?
    a. Red Bays Island
    b. the Bahamas Islands
    c. Andros Island
    d. Ellis Island

3. Define "manumitted":
    a. Freed from slavery
    b. Married
    c. Graduated
    d. Mute

4. How did slaves on ships gain their freedom?
    a. If their ship docked in the British West Indies
    b. If they mutinied and landed in the territory where slavery was illegal
    c. If they crashed and were rescued by British sailors
    d. All of the above

5. Who was Madison Washington?
    a. The leader of a ship who landed in the British West Indies and freed everyone
    b. A slave who helped incite the most successful slave revolt in American history
    c. A cook who mutinied onboard his ship and landed in the British West Indies
    d. All of the above

6. What was the Gold Rush?
    a. When the American economy collapsed
    b. When both the North and the South tried to make as much money as possible before the war
    c. When huge amounts of gold were found in California
    d. When massive amounts of gold were discovered in Latin America

7. What were some of the characteristics of the Sacramento River area during the Gold Rush?
    a. A few blacks had struck it rich
    b. The free black community in Sacramento was strong and organized
    c. The free blacks established, hotels, businesses, restaurants, a newspaper and helped to fund the Underground Railroad
    d. All of the above

8. TRUE or FALSE: Many African American found freedom in the slave free state of California and were prosperous as part of the Gold Rush?
    a. True
    b. False

9. What purpose was served by the Black National Conventions of the 19th Century?
    a. They provided a forum where free African Americans could strategize on their concerns and impatience with the current political system's position on the abolition of slavery
    b. They provided a place where African Americans could gather and boast to how well the slaves were being treated
    c. They provides an opportunity to share their happiness and content with slavery
    d. They provided a place where they could freely drink, dance and be merry

ANTEBELLUM AND THE CIVIL WAR, 1801-1865

CHAPTER 3

HEROISM

The wars of this time period showcased the bravery and heroism of the many African American men who fought for the United States and also for the British as these soldiers searched for a way to advance the opportunities of their own community.

Simultaneously, as the country came into its own, there continued to be push-back for the immoral holding of slaves. During this time, there were a number of slave revolts orchestrated by African American men and women, who advocated for their own freedom and attempted to take it through organization and armed insurrection.

One such example is Denmark Vesey, a carpenter in South Carolina who had purchased his freedom by winning the lottery for $600. However, he was unable to buy the freedom of his wife and children, which many say gave him his unwavering commitment to abolishing slavery. Vesey became well-known in the local church and began preaching to the African American community about how they were similar to the Israelites in the Old Testament, in spite of the monitoring of white authorities.

Vesey eventually began plotting a slave-led rebellion with other members of the church. Their plan sought to kill the governor of Charleston, seize the city's weapons, set fire to the city, and seek revenge on every white man in the city. However, slaves who were nervous that the plan would fail told their masters. Vesey was arrested and hanged. Although his story ends tragically and unjustly, Vesey became a symbol of African American resilience and the abolitionist movement.

Similarly, and potentially inspired by Vesey's boldness, Nat Turner incited a slave rebellion in Virginia in 1831. Turner was a religious and highly intelligent African American man. He gained a following of other enslaved African Americans in his community in Southampton County, which was a plantation area comprised mainly of slaves. Turner coordinated with his fellow slaves, planning their revolt for months. Finally, on the day of a solar eclipse, Turner communicated with his fellow slaves through song and whistles. They began by traveling from house to house, killing any white people with the use of knives and hatchets as opposed to firearms. This successful uprising resulted in the death of approximately 60 white men, women, and children. Turner hid from authorities in the woods but was eventually found and hanged. Turner's bravery and organization with his fellow slaves also ended tragically, but it did strengthen abolitionist arguments. And backlash, as white slave owners became hysterically terrified of slave revolts and sought the passage of laws further limiting the freedom of African Americans.

In July 1839, 53 Africans – enslaved in Sierra Leone, and in transit to plantation owners in Havana, Cuba – broke free from their captors, took over the slave ship *La Amistad* (Spanish for "Friendship"), and ordered the survivors to sail the ship back to

Africa. Instead, they were sailed to the north and eventually were captured off the coast of Long Island by the *USS Washington*. The owners of the ship, and the Spanish government claimed them as property to be returned, while the United States argued that they were legally free since both the United States and Great Britain had banned the trans-Atlantic slave trade in 1808. The case got appealed to the U.S. Supreme Court, and in 1841, in a rare Federal-level court victory for African-Americans in the 1800s, the survivors were ordered to be freed, since they had been illegally transported and acted in self-defense. In 1842, helped by funds raised by the United Missionary Society, 35 survivors were returned to Africa.

A few years later, in 1850, the Fugitive Slave Act made the return of escaped slaves into law and thwarted these brave individual's attempts to find freedom. As one result, the Underground Railroad was founded to help fugitives avoid being returned to slavery under the Fugitive Slave Act. The Underground Railroad using secret meeting points, routes, transportation, and safe houses, orchestrated by former slaves and white and black abolitionists helped slaves escape to freedom. The slaves escaped to Free states, Canada and Nova Scotia. Some of the Underground Railroad members included free African Americans, Quakers, Presbyterians, Methodists, and more. The Underground Railroad had many notable participants, including John Fairfield, the son of a slaveholding family, who made many daring rescues, Levi Coffin, a Quaker who ran a Sunday school for blacks which was heavily opposed and subsequently forced to close. Levi Coffin wrote, "Both my parents and grandparents were opposed to slavery, and none of either of the families ever owned slaves; and all were friends of the oppressed, so I claim that I inherited my anti-slavery principles." Questioned about why he aided slaves, Coffin said "The Bible, in bidding us to feed the hungry and clothe the naked, said nothing about color, and I should try to follow out the teachings of that good book. The many whites who were strongly against slavery held to a common thread, "to be successful; revolutionary change requires people of action — those who little by little chip away at the forces who stand in the way". The sentiment of "conductors" of the Underground Railroad and those who risk their lives by housing and caring for blacks during their transport were not content to wait for laws to change or for slavery to implode itself; railroad activists helped individual fugitive slaves find the road to freedom. Harriet Tubman born a slave herself and having freed her own family by way of the railroad was perhaps the most famous "conductor". Together those active in the Underground Railroad freed more than 100,000 slaves between 1830-1871. All of the people involved in the Underground Railroad regardless of their role or race - may be considered heroes.

CHAPTER REVIEW

1. Who was Levi Coffin?
 a. A Quaker
 b. An abolitionist
 c. An individual active in the Underground Railroad
 d. All of the above

2. Why did Denmark Vesey, a man who had bought his own freedom, have an unwavering commitment to abolish slavery?
 a. He wanted revenge
 b. He was unable to buy the freedom for his wife and children
 c. He hated all white people
 d. He wasn't very smart

3. Who is Nat Turner?
    a. A slave who organized the bloodiest slave revolt in American history
    b. A white landowner who was particularly cruel to his slaves
    c. A preacher who organized a failed slave revolt
    d. The founder of the Underground Railroad

4. Approximately how many white people were killed during Nat Turner's Rebellion?
    a. 50
    b. 60
    c. 70
    d. 80

5. How many African Americans did the Underground Railroad liberate approximately?
    a. 10
    b. 100
    c. 100,000
    d. 10,000

6. Harriet Tubman was active in which movements?
    a. Abolition
    b. Feminism
    c. The Civil War
    d. All of the Above

7. Why did Denmark Vesey hang for the 1822 slave revolt that never happened?
    a. The plans were spoiled by nervous and fearful members
    b. He did not have a well thought out plan
    c. The members of his church did want to see the governor of Charleston killed
    d. He ran away and refused to confess to planning the revolt

ANTEBELLUM AND THE CIVIL WAR, 1801-1865

CHAPTER 4

ART

This period of art for African Americans was a time of new mediums, including photography and sculpture, and new practitioners in those mediums. One such example is the photographer and abolitionist James Presley Ball, Sr. (1825-1904). Ball was born as a freedman in Virginia. He trained in the daguerreotype, which was a form of early photography that depicted portraits of its subjects. He took photographs of notable Americans and did a tour throughout the country, publishing his massive collection of photographs from the journey. His photos depicted plantations, the slave trade, Niagara Falls, and many other social and natural features of the country.

Similarly, Patrick H. Reason (1812-1898) was an engraver, lithographer, and an active abolitionist. He was born in New York City as a freedman and gained an apprenticeship to an English engraver in the city. His own work often took up anti-slavery themes, such as his infamous image of a kneeling slave that was used in abolitionist literature for a century. He undertook many other famous engravings, such as the portrait of a senator, and works in prominent abolitionist books. He opened a shop and achieved great success selling his engravings to the wider public.

Other mediums also drew a strong African American group of influencers, such as painting and sculpture. Edward Mitchell Bannister was a prominent landscape painter, depicting pastoralism. Born in Canada, Bannister moved to New England when he was approximately twenty years old, and he began to make an impression on the art scenes of Boston, Providence, and New York City. His landscapes were complemented by portraits and depictions of biblical scenes. His works became symbolic of the latent talent of African American painters.

Robert Seldon Duncanson (1821-1872) was also a prominent painter during this period who contributed to landscape painting in the United States. His paintings stunned audiences as he contributed to multiple flourishing forms of artwork. Born in New York, Duncanson was born to free parents. His father often worked as a painter and a carpenter, which is where Duncanson most likely first began to paint. He gained apprenticeships and established a successful business. However, Duncanson left his life in New York to pursue his dream of fine arts in Cincinnati, Ohio. Duncanson effectively taught himself how to paint and sketch, using prints and copying engravings. After having some success in portraiture, he began working on landscapes. The results were breathtaking and attracted abolitionists as patrons who supported his success.

Several African American women were also prominent artists during this time period as well. Harriet Powers (1837-1910) stands out as a prominent folk artist during this period, sewing some of the most beautiful quilts to come from this time period.

Powers was born into slavery in Georgia, where she learned how to sew. Biblical stories inspired her work, which she began to exhibit her quilts at county fairs. Her two most famous quilts, Bible Quilt, and Pictorial Quilt were some of the most beautiful and unique pieces of artwork during this period, as they both told an elaborate story and showed her technical skill.

Edmonia Lewis was another prominent African American artist who worked as a sculptor. Born in New York, Lewis was notably talented at a young age in sculpture and other arts. Though she spent most of her career in Italy, Lewis continued to incorporate themes relevant to African Americans in her work and became the first African American woman to achieve international fame in this field.

CHAPTER REVIEW

1. What medium did James Presley Ball, Sr. work with?
    a. Photography
    b. Lithography
    c. Daguerreotypes
    d. All of the above

2. What was one of Patrick H. Reason's most famous engravings?
    a. The portrait of a senator
    b. The image of a kneeling slave
    c. His engravings in books
    d. His image of Uncle Tom's Cabin

3. Edward Mitchell Bannister worked on what type of paintings most prominently?
    a. Portraits
    b. Landscapes
    c. Political cartoons
    d. Biblical

4. Robert Seldon Duncanson worked on what types of paintings most prominently?
    a. Portraits
    b. Landscapes
    c. Political cartoons
    d. Biblical

5. What style of artwork did Harriet Powers produce?
    a. Folk art
    b. The Hudson School of Art
    c. Critical Realism
    d. Traditional art

6. Harriet Powers depicted which types of scenes?
    a. Portraits
    b. Landscapes
    c. Political cartoons
    d. Biblical

7. Where was Edmonia Lewis the most famous and in what medium?
    a. London, photography
    b. Italy, sculpture
    c. France, daguerreotypes
    d. United States, sculpture

CHAPTER 5

LITERATURE

Frederick Douglass (née Frederick Augustus Washington Bailey) was born a slave in the state of Maryland in 1818. After his escape from slavery at the age of 20, Douglass became a renowned abolitionist, editor, and feminist. Douglass traveled widely, and often to lecture against slavery. His first of three autobiographies, *The Narrative of the Life of Frederick Douglass: An American Slave*, was published in 1845. By 1830, there were more than 50 Negro abolitionists' organizations across the country. In 1847 Douglas moved to Rochester, New York, and started working with fellow abolitionist Martin R. Delany to publish a weekly anti-slavery newspaper, *North Star*. Douglass was a signer of the Declaration of Sentiments; he also promoted woman suffrage in his *North Star*. He authored 280 books.

In 1870 Douglass launched The New National Era out of Washington, D.C. He was nominated for vice-president by the Equal Rights Party to run with Victoria Woodhull as a presidential candidate in 1872. He became U.S. marshal of the District of Columbia in 1877. His home in the District of Columbia is a national historic site.

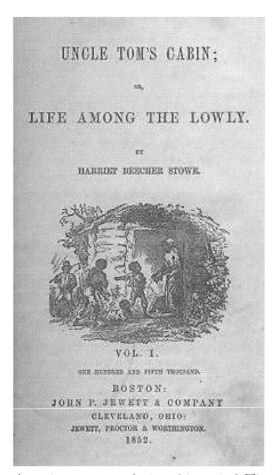

Literature during this time was a powerful testament to the mounting physical, spiritual, and emotional toll slavery had taken on African American communities. As one of the most important works of this time, *Uncle Tom's Cabin* (1852), written by Harriet Beecher Stowe, told the story of a slave and his difficult life. Her sentimental novel became the second-best selling book of that century, following the *Bible*.

During this period, Sojourner Truth escaped slavery and used her writings to, not only discuss her life but also to push for the freedom of African Americans. Her speeches, and her novel *Narrative of Sojourner Truth* were some of the most important and prominent works written by an African American woman during this period. The truth was born into slavery in New York but managed to escape with her daughter to freedom in 1826, leaving her son behind. Yet, in 1828, Truth took her son's owner to court to win him back and won, making her the first black women to win such a case against a white man. She went on to join feminists and abolitionists during this period, making her most famous speech in 1851 at the Ohio Women's Rights Convention. Titled "Ain't I A Woman?" it advocated for the recognition by white men and women of the ongoing struggle of black women. She spoke in the dialect of the time and played off of the theme of British abolitionists, who would commonly use the phrase, "Am I Not a Man and a Brother?" to advocate for liberation. Truth was a powerful advocate for abolition and has been named one of the top 100 most influential people of all time by the Smithsonian Institute.

The Freedom's Journal was the first African American owned and operation newspaper in America. "We wish to plead our own cause. Too long have others spoken for us. Too long has the public been deceived by misrepresentations, in things which concern us dearly . . . ." In March 12, 1827. The founders of *Freedom's Journal*, John B. Russwurm and Samuel Cornish, stated in their masthead that the paper was "devoted to the improvement of the colored population." They noted that blacks had been "incorrectly represented by the press and the church. Their faults were always noted but their virtues remain unmentioned." There were 500,000 free persons of color in the U.S. and they anticipated that at least half of them would read the journal. The paper was published until 1830. Copies of the newspaper can still be found in the Library of Congress on microfilm.

In 1827, David Walker published "An Appeal to the Coloured Citizens of the World." David Walker was born in Wilmington North Carolina, although his father was enslaved his mother was free, therefore, he was a free man. Early on he became affiliated with the African Methodist Episcopal Church activists. Having witness horrific atrocities to African Americans on account of racism and discrimination, including a case where a son was forced to whip his mother to death. In his appeal he urged African Americans to unite and fight for their freedom and equality. While the Appeal frightened many who feared repercussion, it also inspired future leaders and activists to stand up and against oppression. Walker advocated and spoke without hesitation on the importance of education, insisting that an educated black man was the white man's worse enemy and greatest fear.

In his appeal he considered slavery to be a sin, stating that God would punish the nation for their transgressions. Walker found the oppression and treatment of fellow blacks unbearable. "If I remain in this bloody land," he later recalled thinking, "I will not live long...I cannot remain where I must hear slaves' chains continually and where I must encounter the insults of their hypocritical enslavers. He argued: "See your Declaration Americans!!! Do you understand your own language? Hear your languages, proclaimed to the world, July 4th, 1776—"We hold these truths to be self-evident-that ALL MEN ARE CREATED EQUAL!! that they are endowed by their Creator with certain unalienable rights; that among these are life, liberty, and the pursuit of happiness!!" Compare your own language above, extracted from your Declaration of Independence, with your cruelties and murders inflicted by your cruel and unmerciful fathers and yourselves on our fathers and on us—men who have never given your fathers or you the least provocation!!!!!!" Walker spoke out publicly and distributed his pamphlets where ever he could, even smuggling them when necessary. He especially aimed to get the appeal in the hands of those enslaved in the south. The appeal also held regular citizens responsible and encouraged them to act on religion and political principals to end slavery, discrimination and racism.

Southern states did respond with Georgia and Louisiana passing legislation that made distribution of the Appeal illegal. Other states banned distribute and imposed harsh punishments to anyone distributing on reading the pamphlet. North Carolina passed a law making it illegal to teach slaves to read. There was also a $10,000 reward offered for Walker, dead or alive.

CHAPTER REVIEW

1. Who wrote *Uncle Tom's Cabin*?
    a. Harriet Tubman
    b. Harriet Powers
    c. Harriet Beecher Stowe
    d. Sojourner Truth

2. What book helped lay the groundwork for the Civil War?
    a. *The Bible*
    b. *The Life and Times of a Slave Girl*
    c. *Uncle Tom's Cabin*
    d. Sojourner Truth's autobiography

3. TRUE or FALSE: Sojourner Truth escaped slavery
    a. True
    b. False

4. Why is Sojourner Truth remembered?
    a. For being the first African American woman to win a court case against a white slave owner
    b. For her oration abilities
    c. For her abolitionist writings
    d. All of the above

5. What is the name of Truth's infamous speech?
    a. "Give Me Liberty or Give Me Death"
    b. "Amazing Grace"
    c. "Ain't I a Woman?"
    d. "Freedom Now"

6. Who was Frederick Douglass?
    a. He was the author of 280 books
    b. He was the publisher of the anti-slavery newspaper the North Star
    c. He was an abolitionist nominated to run as vice-president in 1872 presidential election
    d. All of the Above

7. TRUE OR FALSE: The Freedom's Journal was created to provide a more accurate depiction of African Americans.
    a. True
    b. False

8. Why was the Appeal such a threat to the southern states in 1827?
    a. The Appeal brought to light the atrocities practiced by the slave owners
    b. The Appeal encouraged all citizen to take responsibility in ending slavery
    c. The Appeal encouraged colored people to fight oppression regardless of risk
    d. All of the above

ANTEBELLUM AND THE CIVIL WAR, 1801-1865

CHAPTER 6

MATH AND SCIENCE

There were several successful African American scientists and mathematicians in this time period. One of note was Charles L Reason (1818-1893), a mathematician, linguist, and a teacher who became the first African American professor. Originally from New York City, Reason was born into a free

family who had migrated to the United States from Haiti after the revolution there. He was recognized as a prodigy in mathematics and began teaching other African Americans at the young age of fourteen. He later founded a society in 1847 for the betterment of African American children, and he created a teaching school as an answer to the charge that black teachers were inefficient and incompetent. His contributions in mathematics earned him continuous employment as a professor in New York. Reason is a striking example of a brilliant African American mathematician who used his talents to benefit his community and other African Americans.

While a man named Reason prevailed in mathematics and teaching, Americans hoped that a different kind of reason would prevail in their country in the aftermath of the Civil War. The Thirteenth Amendment was written, bringing the system of slavery to an end – one of the main goals of the abolitionists in the North in the Civil War.

The Thirteen Amendment was approved by 2/3 of the states for ratification and added to the *United States Constitution*. A nation ripped apart by Civil War, and recovering from over 600,000 dead, hoped it could somehow unite and heal, under the words of the Thirteenth Amendment:

Section 1. Neither slavery nor involuntary servitude, except as a punishment for crime whereof the party shall have been duly convicted, shall exist within the United States, or any place subject to their jurisdiction.

Section 2. Congress shall have the power to enforce this article by appropriate legislation.

CHAPTER REVIEW

1. Who was Charles L. Reason?
    a. A mathematician
    b. The founder of a society to advance the interests of African American children
    c. The first African American university professor
    d. All of the above

2. When did Reason found his society?
    a. 1850
    b. 1849
    c. 1848
    d. 1847

3. Why is Reason an example of an exceptional African American?
    a. He was a prodigy in mathematics
    b. He used his talents to benefit his community
    c. He gained longstanding and pioneering teaching positions
    d. All of the above

AFRICAN AMERICAN HISTORY
ADDITIONAL REFERENCES … AND FOR A "DEEPER DIVE"

Sojourner Truth: A Life, A Symbol

By *Nell Irvin Painter*

Black Cow Boys Of The West

By *Tricia Martineau Wagner*

Harriet, The Moses Of Her People

By *Sarah Hopkins Bradford*

Let Him Know That You Are A Man

By *Isaac J. Hill*

African American Faces Of The Civil War: An Album

By *Ronald S. Coddington*

Black Fortunes: The Story Of The First Six African Americans Who Escaped Slavery And Became Millionaires

By *Shomari Wills*

Narrative Of The Life Of Frederick Douglass

By *Frederick Douglass*

The Original Black Elite: Daniel Murray And The Story Of A Forgotten Era

By *Elizabeth Dowling Taylor*

Tell Them We Are Rising: The Story Of Historically Black Colleges And Universities Stanley Nelson (Director)

Rated: PG

Format: DVD

American Experience: The Abolitionists.

Rated: PG

Format: DVD

Black Gun, Silver Star: The Life And Legend Of Frontier Marshal Bass Reeves (Race And Ethnicity In The American West)

By Art T. Burton

Twelve Years A Slave By Solomon Northup (Author), Henry Louis Gates (Editor, Afterword), Ira Berlin (Introduction), & 1 More

Up From Slavery

By Booker T. Washington

Black Officer In A Buffalo Soldier Regiment: The Military Career Of Charles Young

By Brian G. Shellum

PERIOD 4 - RECONSTRUCTION 1866-1900

RECONSTRUCTION 1866 - 1900

CHAPTER 1

ABRAHAM LINCOLN SPEAKS

I was sitting in a chair in the right box, enjoying the play "Our American Cousin" at Ford's Theater, when John Wilkes Booth pulled out a gun and killed me on the night of April 14, 1865. My name is Abraham Lincoln, and I guess you could say I'm the dead white man in this story.

A lot has been said about me and my position on slavery over the years, so I thought I'd take a few moments to set the record straight. The truth is, if you look carefully, you can find something about me being opposed to slavery in each decade of my life.

My father decided to move us from Kentucky to Indiana in 1816 to get us away from slavery. When I was nineteen, in 1828, I brought produce down the Mississippi to New Orleans and saw slave markets for the first time. Seven Negroes attacked and tried to rob us, but we escaped them on our flatboat. Maybe if that hadn't happened, I might have been more sympathetic a bit sooner.

But less than 10 years later, in 1837, I and Dan Stone were the only two state legislators in Illinois to stand against slavery, calling it "an injustice."

In a letter to Joshua Speed, I recalled an 1841 expedition we had on a steamboat going from Louisville to St. Louis and wrote this to him: "You may remember, as well as I do, that... there were, on board, ten or a dozen slaves, shackled together with irons. That sight was a continual torment to me which has, and continually exercises, the power of making me miserable." In the late 1840s, I introduced a bill in Congress to outlaw slavery in the District of Columbia, as I was tired of seeing slaves treated like droves of horses. The bill failed, as did my attempt to get a second term in Congress.

You may remember the debates I had with Stephen A. Douglas for the Presidency. You may not recall that it was the role of Douglas in getting that pro-slavery Kansas-Nebraska Act passed, that made me say this in 1854, because I was against the expansion of slavery: "It is wrong...wrong in its...effect, letting slavery into Kansas and Nebraska - and wrong in ...principle, allowing it to spread to every other part of the wide world, where men can be found inclined to take it...When we were the political slaves of King George, and wanted to be free, we called the maxim that 'all men are created equal' a self-evident truth; but now when we have grown fat, and have lost the dread of being slaves ourselves, we have become so greedy as *masters* that we call the same a 'self-evident lie.'"

In a speech on February 21, 1861, while running for President, I called the Declaration of Independence "that which gave promise in due time the weights should be lifted from the shoulders of all men, and that *all* should have an equal chance."

I always hinted at my support of the end of this heinous cancer on our nation, called slavery. I wrote the Emancipation Proclamation and released it when I felt the time was right.

But it's also fair to say my main goal was to keep us together as a nation. I didn't want it to be all slave but did say I believed it someday was going to go all one way, or all the other: "A house divided against itself cannot stand," and all that. Had the North lost the Civil War, it might have gone in the other direction. Had we lost the American Revolution and stayed British colonies, our Civil War might have happened earlier, in the 1820s, when Britain banned slavery. It's always easy to play "what could have happened" with American history.

Now I'm not this perfect person to put up on some pedestal in a grand monument - in my youth, I often joked about and made fun of the slaves, even convinced myself at times that they were enjoying their lot in life. I had to make compromises to bring the nation back together, like giving land to black landowners in the South, but not immediately giving them the vote. I'm ashamed of some of it but know I came through for many, in ways that it counted.

I am on a train now, my body rolling across the nation in a coffin draped with the Stars and Stripes. All these miles, and I have never seen so many African Americans in my life as I sense now, lining up all across America to give me one last look.

Now I don't know what will happen to this nation, or if it will forever stay together, but I take solace in the fact that in my short time on earth, I did something right, something lasting, and something good for the children of the children I am sensing now. I lost children, my wife is despondent, and I cannot console her. There has been so much tragedy in my life; the only good thing I can say about my death is that all the tragedy is finally over.

I didn't mean to leave you all so soon - but I hope you will remember me, and maybe sometimes read some of the words I've left behind for you.

RECONSTRUCTION BEGINS

The period following the 1861-1865 Civil War is commonly referred to as *Reconstruction* because it refers to both the rebuilding of the country following the Civil War and the restructuring of the Southern states which had attempted to leave the Union. This rebuilding was an extensive, expensive, and complicated process that attempted to both help the country heal while creating new norms for the treatment of African Americans.

When Abraham Lincoln was assassinated in 1865, the process of Reconstruction was thrown into chaos. The turmoil and debate the resulted from how to rebuild the Southern governments while maintaining order divided the government and threw the country into an intensive debate. Adding to the turmoil, the South suffered complete economic and material destruction. Eleven major cities were severely damaged or completely destroyed by the Union during the war, including Atlanta, Charleston, Columbia, and Richmond. The problems were numerable that faced the unprepared President Andrew Johnson.

Some of our brave colored Boys who helped to free Cuba.

Instead of honoring the promises of Union army officials and President Lincoln, President Johnson reversed Special Field Order No. 15 of General William Tecumseh Sherman and ordered that all land be returned to Southern property owners instead of freed African Americans. This policy of Reconstruction resulted in a system of sharecropping, or a system where a tenant farmer cultivates farmland by giving a part of each crop as rent to a landholder. In this system, black tenants (and poor white Americans, who also worked as sharecroppers) were unable to ever earn enough money to purchase tools, seeds, land, or even to move to a different state. Because of this system, both were commonly kept in poverty.

In 1866, Congress passed legislation that enabled African Americans to formally enlist in the country's peacetime military. This lead to the creation of the Buffalo Soldiers, which included two regiments of all-African American troops, the 9th and 10th cavalries, as well as the creation of four African American infantry regiments. For over two decades in the late 1800s, these troops engaged in military campaigns against hostile Native Americans on the Plains and along the southwest. The African American soldiers played a leading role in aiding the United States in its westward expansion. Their roles included protecting settlers, building forts and roads, capturing horse and cattle thieves, and protecting the U.S. Mail, stagecoaches, and wagon trains. The troops were among the 180,000 African Americans who served the Union side of the Civil War. They were respected by the Native Americans for their courage and ferocity in battle and may have earned the name Buffalo Soldiers out of that respect. Eighteen

Buffalo Soldiers received the Medal of Honor for their bravery in dealing with the rugged western terrain and its challenges. That success reduced the resistance toward the idea of African American soldiers and officers and paved the way for the first African American graduate of West Point in 1877.

There were other gains for equality during this time. In 1866 the Civil Rights Bill was passed, giving every American citizenship before the law regardless of race. At first, Johnson vetoed the bill using his presidential powers, but Congress used their Constitutional powers to overrule his veto by gaining a two-thirds majority. This was the first time that the U.S. Congress had used their overruling powers to reject a presidential veto. This law eventually became the Fourteenth Amendment, which provided equal protection, citizenship, and a bill of rights to all Americans.

The Fourteen Amendment was contradicted in myriad ways in local law throughout the South, such as the Black Codes. The Black Codes were laws passed by Southern states during Reconstruction, to further restrict the freedom of African Americans and confine them to similar systems of slavery.

To continue maintaining control of Congress, anti-slavery members of the government strove to enforce the enfranchisement of black men but again were met with an unwillingness on the local level to honor these laws. African American men faced continuous barriers to voting, and African American women did not have the right to vote at all.

By 1877, Northern support for reconstruction and promoting equality had waned, in part due to an economic downturn. A contested Presidential election the year before pushed the two political parties to make a severe compromise in order to elect the President. In this compromise, the Northern states effectively agreed to pull troops out of the South and cease any and all oversight, effectively killing Reconstruction and vastly limiting the possibility for meaningful change. This, coupled with the active efforts of the Klu Klux Klan, a terrorist organization designed to use violence to suppress the black vote and keep African Americans oppressed, made the African American political situation dire.

This lack of accountability enabled Southern states to reinforce racist laws and to pass what is known as the Jim Crow laws, which were regulations that barred black American from accessing equal rights. These laws created *segregation*, keeping black and white Americans separate. This period further entrenched many of the battles that African Americans believed were settled with the Civil War and the policies of reconstruction. However, with a lack of political will, the country continued to refuse to move forward.

CHAPTER REVIEW

1. "Reconstruction" can be defined as:
    a. Rebuilding after damage or destruction
    b. The period following the Civil War in the United States
    c. A policy to restore the country and the Southern United States
    d. All of the above

2. Reconstruction was aimed at:
    a. Rebuilding the country overall and restructuring the southern United States
    b. Rebuilding the country overall and restructuring the northern United States
    c. Rebuilding the South after the Civil War and restructuring the North
    d. Rebuilding the country overall

3. What killed the dream of reconstruction?
    a. An economic downturn
    b. The northern states pulled needed troops out of the south
    c. The terrorist effects of the KKK
    d. All of the above

4. When was President Lincoln assassinated?
    a. 1861
    b. 1863
    c. 1865
    d. 1867

5. "Sharecropping" is:
    a. A system wherein a tenant farmer cultivates the land and gives a part of each crop as rent to the landholder
    b. Upheld the same systems of oppression as slavery
    c. Was practiced by both black and white Americans
    d. All of the above

6. The first time the U.S. Congress overruled a presidential veto was to pass which bill into law?
    a. The Emancipation Proclamation
    b. The Equal Land Act of 1866
    c. The Civil Rights Bill of 1866
    d. None of the Above

7. What majority is required by Congress to overrule a presidential veto?
    a. 1/3
    b. 1/2
    c. 2/3
    d. unanimous

RECONSTRUCTION 1866 - 1900

CHAPTER 2
RESILIENCE

In order to practice their newfound rights, many African Americans rallied to both enjoy and expand their freedoms. They staged sit-ins, participated in elections, and formed political associations to rally their power. This translated to approximately 2,000 African American men holding office during the period of Reconstruction. Although these office holders drastically improved the inequality that plagued the country, their efforts were simply the beginning of a lengthy process that would continue into the 20th and 21st centuries.

Just as occurred during the antebellum period, African Americans founded communities of resilience in all of the new corners of the greatly-expanded country. As one striking example, many African Americans became cowboys in the American West. In fact, approximately 25% of all cowboys were African American, as many were former slaves who had gained skills in working with cattle. By the end of the Civil War, many made their way West and were met with far less discrimination than existed in the Northeast or the South.

There were many notable African American cowboys, such as Addison Jones (1845-1926). Jones was born in Texas and grew up working with cattle. While working with a group of all black cowboys, Jones became known for excelling in all areas of his field, such as bronc riding and managing cattle in all kinds of situations. He knew many skills, as well as tricks, and had a perfect sense of timing while working with his animals. He eventually married a cook at an inn in New Mexico, but he continued his work, spreading fame at his talent and reliability throughout the Southwest.

Mary Fields (1832-1914) was one of the most infamous female cowboys in the history of the

American West. Fields was originally born a slave in 1832 in Tennessee. After the Civil War and the Emancipation Proclamation, Fields found work. In 1884, her aunt—a nun—was sent to Montana to establish a school for an indigenous community. While there, Fields's aunt fell extremely ill with pneumonia. When Fields heard of this, she immediately rushed to Montana to take care of her aunt. Fields worked any job that she could and even opened a restaurant at one point. However, when she was nearly sixty years old, the

United States Postal Service (USPS) hired her to carry mail throughout the region, using a team of six horses. Fields became the first African American woman to work for the USPS. Her reliability earned her the respect of everyone around her, as even in heavy snowfall, Fields could be counted on to deliver the mail. Her successful career earned her the nickname "Stagecoach Mary."

Bass Reeves (1838-1910) was a notorious cowboy, said to be the real Lone Ranger, who became one of the most important U.S. Marshals in Oklahoma. Reeves was born into slavery in Arkansas and worked on the Reeve's farm, during the Civil War while working as a servant to George, the son of William Reeves, he beat up George to escape slavery and fled to Indian Territory where he lived and learned the languages of the Cherokee, Seminoles and Creek Indians until he was legally freed through emancipation. Upon the issuance of the Emancipation Proclamation, Reeves was able to take up farming. He lived as a farmer with his wife and ten children, until word of his skills with Native American languages spread. Because of this, he was recruited by a local sheriff to work as a deputy. He was the first black deputy marshal in the Western United States. During his work, his reputation for justice and skill spread throughout the region. He became a legend during his lifetime and was a known marksman with the ability to accurately shoot a raffle or hand gun from either hand. He was also a skilled detective and is credited with the arrests of over 3000 criminals, bringing in some of the most dangerous and notorious criminals of the time, as he managed to survive many gunfights. A bronze statue of Reeves was erected in Pendergraft Park Fort Smith Arkansas.

Yet, African Americans were more than just cowboys, upholders of the law, and politicians. African American communities also had begun to cultivate their own systems and sites of resilience, such as occurred at Tuskegee University. This private and historically black university, located in Alabama, was founded by Booker T. Washington and Lewis Adams after the Civil War in 1881. The university became a widespread site for educating and cultivating black talent. Tuskegee students studied topics from engineering to medicine to the arts. It was also a site which allowed notable African American professionals to contribute to the education of younger generations. Education was valued with high regard and esteemed for being the most direct route to a better life.

Benjamin Davis Oliver Sr. – 1880-197, trained as a cadet in high school starting out as a first lieutenant in the Spanish-American war. He moved up the ranks slowly becoming the first black colonel in 1930 and being promoted to general at the age of sixty. He battled segregation by implementing plans for the desegregation of U.S. combat forces during World War II. He taught as a professor of Military Science at both Tuskegee and Wilberforce between 1929 and 1938.

AFRICAN AMERICAN HISTORY

CHAPTER REVIEW

1. What percentage of cowboys were African Americans?
    a. 2.5%
    b. 10%
    c. 25%
    d. 50%

2. What was Addison Jones know for?
    a. Being a famous cowboy
    b. Bronco riding
    c. A skilled cattle rancher
    d. All of the above

3. Who was Mary Fields?
    a. At age sixty, she became the first African American woman to work for the USPS
    b. An African American cowboy/ cowgirl
    c. A well respected and reliable woman mail carrier
    d. All of the above

4. Why did Mary Fields receive the nickname "Stagecoach Mary"?
    a. For her steadfast service to the USPS
    b. Because of her skill with horses
    c. For her many skills with driving
    d. For her work at a local restaurant

5. What was Bass Reeves remembered for?
    a. For being the real "Lone Ranger"
    b. For being skilled in Native American languages
    c. For being the first African American marshal deputy
    d. All of the above

6. What is Tuskegee University?
    a. A historically black university
    b. A university founded by Lewis Adams and Booker T. Washington
    c. A space where African American students could learn a wide variety of disciplines
    d. All of the above

RECONSTRUCTION 1866 - 1900

CHAPTER 3

HEROISM

During this period of massive change, there were many important African American heroes. They helped to found universities, helped to secure more equal rights, placed pressure on politicians, and were the first ones to do the many things that African Americans often were barred from doing during this period.

One of the greatest of these heroes is Frederick Douglass (1818-1895). Douglass was born in  Maryland as a slave. He was separated from his mother and grandmother because his owner sold him. He gradually learned how to read and write with the help of his owner's wife. He used his knowledge to teach fellow slaves to read as well, which caused word to spread that he could teach literacy. He taught as many as 40 African Americans at once. However, when white slave owners caught word of this, they ended the lessons, and Douglass was sold at a young age to a poor farmer with a reputation for extreme violence against his slaves. During this time, Douglass was psychologically abused and physically beaten. He stood up for himself, and bested his owner in a physical confrontation, causing his owner to never try to beat Douglass again. Douglass began attempting to escape slavery. He tried twice before succeeding by taking a train from Philadelphia.

Upon becoming free, Douglass married and took up preaching. Most notably, he began to write his famous autobiography *Narrative of the Life of Frederick Douglass, an American Slave*. His book became a bestseller for its enrapturing plot and beautiful language that described the brutality he had faced as a slave. He used the funds he received from his book to legally purchase his freedom. He then traveled to Ireland and Great Britain, making speeches and exploring the countries while meeting British abolitionists. He then laid plans to begin publishing a newspaper focused on abolition, which he named *The North Star*. He also supported women's suffrage and attended notable suffrage meetings, such as the Seneca Falls Convention.

The Civil War changed everything for Douglass, as he took an extremely active role, from urging

President Lincoln to include African Americans in the armed forces fighting for emancipation to discussing suffrage with Andrew Johnson. Douglass urged suffrage, fighting for equality and came to occupy important roles in African American communities. He was a symbol of African American strength and intellect and is an American hero.

Building on his success, William Edward Burghardt (W.E.B.) Du Bois (1868-1963) was also one of the most important African American heroes of this time. Du Bois was born in Massachusetts. His great grandmother had been a slave, but his family enjoyed some economic success. Du Bois attended Fisk University, located in Tennessee. This was Du Bois's first experience in the South, with Jim Crow and all of the other manifestations of white supremacism. Following this, he attended Harvard University to study sociology and later became the first African American to earn a Ph.D. from Harvard. He also worked at the Tuskegee Institute, eventually becoming the director of the esteemed institution, where he later came to believe that integration was the only thing that would solve the problem of racism in the United States. He organized many pro-African American conferences and movements and also organized against another prominent African American, named Booker T. Washington, who had embraced segregation as a pathway towards equality.

Learning about violent lynching in the South, in which white men and women would torture, mutilate, murder, and hang African Americans in mass mobs, Du Bois became further motivated to action. In response to these horrific events and to Washington, he wrote *The Souls of Black Folk*, a major text about the social experience of being black in America. The book discussed identity and the idea of a "color line" that separated African Americans psychologically, keeping them from achieving their potential as human beings. The book quickly became a foundational piece of literature in the United States. Du Bois continued to write about the experience of African Americans, as well as to critically comment on the mass violence that black communities faced. He did so in part through his work at the National Association for the Advancement of Colored People (NAACP), an association that was formed to bring African Americans together to fight for Civil Rights that Du Bois helped found. One of his writings helped to inspire an initiative in 1911 that outlawed lynching.

On May 23, 1900, Sergeant William H. Carney became the first African American to be presented a Congressional Medal of Honor, for his service to the 54th Massachusetts Infantry, a company largely composed of freed slaves from New York, Massachusetts, Indiana, and as far away as Canada and the Caribbean. These troops banded together in the hope of bringing the Civil War to an end, and with that, the end of slavery, and the hope for new opportunities that would bring them and their families a more promising future.

Mary McLeod Bethune 1875-1955, was an educator, civil rights leader, and adviser to five U.S. presidents who gave African Americans a voice in Washington. She turned her passion for racial progress and organization savvy into the enduring legacies of Bethune-Cookman University and the National Council of Negro Women. She founded and served on many boards.

Bethune was a friend of Eleanor Roosevelt. In in 1936, she became the highest-ranking African American woman in government and was elected director of Negro Affairs of the National Youth Administration by President Franklin Roosevelt. She was also a leader of FDR's unofficial "black cabinet." In 1937, she organized a conference on the Problems of the Negro and Negro Youth and fought to end discrimination and lynching.

Eugene Jacques Bullard's, 1895–1961, life is surrounded by many legends. Born in Columbus Georgia, he was the seventh of ten children. He was said to have witnessed his father's narrow escape from lynching at an early age. His father had spoken about the better opportunities a black could experience in Paris, as a teenager, he stowed away on a German freighter Marta Russ, to escape racial discrimination. World War I began in 1914, and Eugene enlisted. He was assigned as a marching gunner serving as part of the Morocco Division which became one of the most decorated units in the French Army. Upon recovering from being seriously wounded, he transferred to the 170th infantry and was cited for his acts of valor and awarded the Croix de Guerre. He later volunteered in the French Air Service as an air gunner where he subsequently went through his initial flight training and received his pilot license, making him the first African American military pilot. When the U.S. entered the war, he applied to an opening for the Lafayette Flying Corps but was not accepted, as only white pilots were accepted. Eugene would go on to receive 15 war metals from France, and in October 1959, he was made a Knight of The Legion of Honor, the highest ranking order and decoration bestowed by France.

After he returned to his love of music, he worked as a drummer and eventually became the owner of his own club, a bar and the operator of a gym, as a result of the popularity of his club, he had many famous friends, like Louis Armstrong, Josephine Baker and others. He would go on to accept a request from the French government to spy on German citizens, as he spoke German and was a decorated serviceman in France. While serving in the 51st Infantry Regiment, he was badly wounded and was able to escape to Spain and then the U.S. He spent most of his time in a New York hospital. His fame in France did not follow him to the United States, at a concert in Lakeland Acres Peekskill he and other concert goers were knocked to the ground and badly beaten by an angry mob, which included members of the state and local law enforcement. The attack was captured on film and can be seen in the 1970 documentary "The Tallest Tree in Our Forest". Bullard was posthumously commissioned a second lieutenant in the U.S. Air Force in 1994, a bronze portrait head of Bullard was donated and can be seen today at the National Air and Space Museum in Washington D.C., created by Eddie Dixon, an African American sculptor.

RECONSTRUCTION 1866 - 1900

CHAPTER REVIEW

1. Mary McLeod Bethune?
    a. Founded Cookman University
    b. Was advisory to five presidents
    c. She organized a conference to fight discrimination and lynching
    d. All of the above

2. Douglass's owner began treating him differently after what incident?
    a. Douglass tried and failed at several attempts to escape
    b. Douglass got the best of his owner in a physical fight
    c. Douglass was found teaching as many as 40 slaves to read
    d. Douglass was found to be content with his situation

3. Douglass used the money he made from his book to purchase:
    a. Tuition to the Tuskegee Institute
    b. A train ticket to Philadelphia
    c. His wife's freedom
    d. His legal freedom

4. Douglass is most famous for writing:
    a. *The Souls of Black Folk*
    b. *Narrative of the Life of Frederick Douglass, an American Slave*
    c. *Uncle Tom's Cabin*
    d. *Incidents in the Life of a Slave Girl*

5. Douglass advised which president about slavery?
    a. Abraham Lincoln
    b. Ulysses S. Grant
    c. Andrew Jackson
    d. All of the above

6. W. E. B. Du Bois helped to found the NAACP and was the first African American to:
    a. Receive a Ph.D. from Harvard
    b. Receive a Ph.D. from Tuskegee
    c. Receive a Ph.D. from Dartmouth
    d. All of the above

7. W. E. B. Du Bois wrote which of the following:
    a. *The Souls of Black Folk*
    b. *Narrative of the Life of Frederick Douglass, an American Slave*
    c. *Uncle Tom's Cabin*
    d. *Incidents in the Life of a Slave Girl*

8. What esteemed military airman was not allowed to fight in World War II for his own country?
    a. Eugene Jacque Bullard
    b. Ahmet Ali
    c. Benjamin Davis Jr.
    d. Lieutenant Lee Archer

RECONSTRUCTION 1866 - 1900

CHAPTER 4

ART

The period of artwork following the Civil War was one that remained obsessed with depicting various battle scenes as a way to make sense of the violence. Because the whole country was pulled to one side or the other, and everyone had remained uncertain as to how the war would turn out, art was a space where this anxiety was expressed. Adding to this, the Civil War was the first armed conflict in the United States where photography was used to document and communicate the War to the public. These images - most notably from a team headed by Matthew Brady - catapulted photography to the front of the art scene in the United States during this time.

African Americans quickly made their mark on this new opportunity for artistic expression. For example, Cornelius Marion Battey (1873-1927) became an influential African American photographer, known for his portraits of African Americans in a pastoralist style. Battey was born in Georgia but moved to Ohio and then New York, where he spent the majority of his

life. He eventually opened his own studio where he shot portraits. One of his most famous photographs was a portrait of Frederick Douglass just two years before his death. Battey became well-known for his style and skill, and he eventually collaborated with the NAACP, taking the portraits of prominent NAACP leaders. These images were printed in *The Crisis*, an important magazine of the time. Battey went on to also photograph white leaders, such as President Calvin Coolidge. He also became the official photographer of the Tuskegee Institute, teaching courses in photography, and also documenting student life.

Similarly, Arthur P. Bedou (1882-1966) was also an extremely successful African American photographer. Bedou was born in New Orleans and taught himself photography. His career was launched in 1900 when a photograph that he had taken of a solar eclipse was met with widespread acclaim. While working at a Tuskegee Institute conference taking photographs, Booker T. Washington took notice of his work and invited him to work as his personal photographer. During this time, Bedou went touring around the country with Washington and interacted with many prominent Americans. He took some of the most famous photos of figures such as Theodore Roosevelt and George Washington Carver. He later opened his own studio in New Orleans.

Using old methods for new styles, Mary A Bell (1873-1941) became an important African American artist during this period. Bell was born in Washington, DC and never studied art, and was thus largely self-taught. Bell's artwork went largely undiscovered until she was around sixty years old when feminist author Gertrude Stein and several others promoted her sketches. Her artwork depicted everyday scenes of Creole and African American culture in the United States.

Outside of the visual arts, African American music had begun to thrive. William Christopher (W.C.) Handy (1873-1958) was one such musician and composer who benefited from this boom. Born in Alabama to a family of ministers, he secretly starting practicing music. He eventually joined a local band and ended up moving to Birmingham. His musical skill allowed him to begin teaching other musicians and to conduct orchestras. He began to compose and created a new harmonic structure as well as a style of singing. He eventually published his compositions and achieved widespread acclaim, eventually being named the Father of Blues.

Another famous African American musician during this post-war period was Scott Joplin (1867-1917). Joplin was born in Arkansas but later moved to Texas where his natural musical skill was noticed and encouraged by his teachers. Joplin went on to work on the railroad but eventually traveled throughout the country developing his style of music. He is credited with being the master of Ragtime, a type of music with a jagged rhythm. He composed over 40 four popular ragtime pieces, as well as several operas. His work heavily influenced jazz and remains popular today. His music embraced aspects of African-American popular heritage while also embracing elements from his formal musical training.

CHAPTER REVIEW

1. What was the period after the Civil War concerned with?
    a. Making sense of the violence the country had just suffered
    b. Taking sides with the North
    c. Inventing a new style
    d. Returning to the past

2. What medium became popular because of the Civil War?
    a. Sculpture
    b. Painting
    c. Photography
    d. Engraving

3. For what medium did Cornelius Marion Battey become famous for using?
    a. Sculpture
    b. Painting
    c. Photography
    d. Engraving

4. For what medium did Arthur P. Bedou become famous for using?
    a. Sculpture
    b. Painting
    c. Photography
    d. Engraving

5. For what medium did Mary A. Bell become famous for using?
    a. Sculpture
    b. Sketches
    c. Photography
    d. Engraving

6. What types of scenes did Mary A. Bell depict?
    a. Creole and African American everyday life
    b. Images of the Reconstruction South
    c. Portraits of prominent African Americans
    d. Portraits of Creole aristocracy

7. Why is William Christopher Handy famous?
    a. Because is known as "The Father of Blues"
    b. Because he invented new styles of singing
    c. Because he invented a new harmonic structure
    d. All of the above

8. Who was Scott Joplin?
    a. A famous composer of symphonies
    b. A master of ragtime music
    c. A forgotten jazz musician
    d. The Father of Blues

CHAPTER 5

LITERATURE

The period of Reconstruction following the Civil War was a time of literary achievement for African Americans. Many African Americans were able to find work as writers more easily, filling new roles as journalists, novelists, playwrights, and more.

Harriet Ann Jacobs (1813-1897) was one such author who used her life experiences and her talent to describe a firsthand account of the black experience in America. Jacobs was born into slavery in North Carolina, where she learned how to read and write. After being traded between owners, Jacobs was sexually harassed by her owner, and her children were enslaved at birth. She eventually managed to escape by hiding in a swamp and living in an attic. She finally made it to Philadelphia and then New York through abolitionist friends. Fearing that she and her brother, who also had escaped, would be returned following the passage of the Fugitive Slave Act of 1850, she moved with

her brother to California in search of the Gold Rush, mentioned earlier in this book.

Jacobs began to write her memoirs in California. The stories of her remembrances as a slave took the form of two books: *A True Tale of Slavery* and *Incidents in the Life of a Slave Girl*, the second published in 1861. Her book captivated her audiences and added to the chorus of voices demanding freedom. That year, the country devolved into a Civil War in order to free African Americans. Yet there were also African American authors who preserved the cultural history of their time by producing literature about their society. For example, Clarissa Minnie Thompson Allen (1859-1941) was a popular fiction writer during this period. She was born in South Carolina and received a decent education. She went on to teach a variety of subjects before moving to Texas, where she continued working as a teacher. During this time, she began to write stories based on wealthy African American families in the South. Her work, such as *A Mountain of Misfortune*, used sensational topics, such as murder and love triangles, to entertain her audiences. Her quick-wittedness and penchant for storytelling made her a widespread hit.

Similarly, Eloise Bibb Thompson (1878-1928) was an African American educator, playwright, poet, and journalist. Thompson was born in Louisiana and trained to teach at the New Orleans University before attending Oberlin and then Howard. She was a noteworthy scholar, as she continued her studies at

Columbia and New York University (NYU). She published multiple works, including a book of poems, while also writing for the *Los Angeles Tribune*, when she then moved to California. She also published multiple plays, one of which was translated into a film script.

As a literary critic and a notable poet, William Stanley Beaumont Braithwaite (1878-1962) was born in Massachusetts. Braithwaite was forced to work to support his family when he was only twelve years old. He then began writing for the *Boston Evening Transcript*, followed by the *Atlantic Monthly*, and *The New York Times*. He went on to hold a professorship at Atlanta University, where he continued his writings, later publishing three volumes of poetry.

These writers represent just a few of the many African American novelists, poets, journalists, and playwrights that were gaining prominence and importance during this period of American history.

CHAPTER REVIEW

1. What were some of the new roles that African Americans began to fill as writers?
    a. Journalists
    b. Playwrights
    c. Critics
    d. All of the above

2. Why did Harriet Ann Jacobs move to California?
    a. To be free of the Fugitive Slave Act
    b. To follow her brother in the Gold Rush
    c. To ensure her freedom
    d. All of the above

3. For which work is Harriet Ann Jacobs known for writing?
    a. *A True Tale of Slavery* and *Incidents in the Life of a Slave Girl*
    b. *A Mountain of Misfortune*
    c. *The Souls of Black Folk*
    d. *Uncle Tom's Cabin*

4. For which work is Clarissa Minnie Thompson Allen known for writing?
    a. *A True Tale of Slavery* and *Incidents in the Life of a Slave Girl*
    b. *A Mountain of Misfortune*
    c. *The Souls of Black Folk*
    d. *Uncle Tom's Cabin*

5. What qualities did Clarissa Minnie Thompson Allen preserve in her writings?
    a. A depiction of the social scene of the time
    b. Images of the war-torn south
    c. Philosophies about the color line
    d. A depiction of her life in enslavement

6. Eloise Bibb Thompson attended which prominent university?
    a. Columbia University
    b. NYU
    c. Howard
    d. All of the above

7. Braithwaite was forced to work to support his family when he was only twelve years old. What paper did he write for?
    a. New York Times
    b. Boston Evening Transcript
    c. Atlantic Monthly
    d. All of the above

CHAPTER 6
MATH AND SCIENCE

One of the most famous African American scientists of all time was George Washington Carver (1860-1943). Carver was born into slavery in Missouri and was separated from his family when he was kidnapped and sold in Kentucky. His owner arranged his return, and he grew up with his family, learning to read and write in the house of his former owner. He eventually enrolled in school and thrived during his studies. However, when he tried to apply to university, he was rejected because of his race. He

eventually bought land in Kansas, where he began experimenting with plants and flowers as well as with agricultural varieties. Feeling restless after just two years, he obtained a loan from the bank and again applied for admission to universities. This time, Carver was successful, rendering him the first African American to enroll at Iowa State University. There, he studied agriculture and botany. He was encouraged by his supervisor to stay on and continue his work as a master's student, which he did. Carver was so successful in his studies that he became the first African American faculty member at the university.

In 1896, Carver was invited to become the department head of the Agriculture Department at the Tuskegee Institute. Carver stayed at the Tuskegee Institute for nearly 50 years, developing research and inventing groundbreaking advances for agriculture. Some of these discoveries included a method to improve the quality of soil depleted by cotton planting, creating new varieties of sweet potatoes and soybeans, and inventing the popular food item peanut butter. His innovation caused him to become famous, and he was also called upon to testify to Congress regarding the peanut industry. He forever changed the sciences for African Americans, as his work became so vital and well-known to scientists everywhere.

Adding to this legacy, Ernest Everett Just (1863-1941) was a groundbreaking scientist who worked primarily in biology. Just was born in South Carolina and was raised by his mother after his father and grandfather both died. Just was eventually sent to New Hampshire to attend the Kimball Union Academy, a preparatory high school. While in school, his mother died, but he managed to graduate in three years instead of four as the valedictorian. He went on to attend Dartmouth and became a distinguished scholar in several fields, such as botany and history. He won nearly every prize offered by the school as well as important scholarships. He went on to find work at Howard University, a historic black university in Washington, D.C. He became the head of the zoology department, where he made great discoveries in embryology.

Roger Arliner Young (1889-1964), a student of Ernest Everett Just, was a prominent African American female zoologist and biologist. Born in Virginia, Young enrolled at Howard University, originally with the intention of studying music. Just took an interest in her, seeing promise in her work.

She went on to study zoology in a graduate program at the University of Chicago but returned to Howard to work with Just. During this time, she worked at the Marine Biological Laboratory in Massachusetts and made discoveries about the fertilization process of marine organisms. After a falling out with Just, she left Howard to teach elsewhere, where she continued to make interesting and vital discoveries in the field of marine biology.

Andrew J. Beard (1849-1921) was born as a slave and became a farmer, carpenter, blacksmith, railroad worker, and inventor of both a rotary steam engine and a device called the Jenny Coupler. The Jenny Coupler automatically linked train cars together by simply allowing them to bump into each other to connect.

Lewis Howard Latimer worked on improving electric light in the 1880s, extending the life of light bulbs, making them more efficient and enabling them to be installed safely in homes and on streets. In addition to his own designs, he worked closely with Thomas Edison, and in 1884, he was hired by the Edison Electric Light Company as a draftsman and expert witness in patent litigation on electric lights. In his long career as a draughtsman, he also worked with Alexander Graham Bell. In 1890, he wrote the first book on electric lighting, *Incandescent Electric Lighting*. He later supervised the installation of public electric lights throughout New York, Philadelphia, Montreal, and London, and oversaw the installation of lighting in railroad stations, government buildings, and major roads in Canada, New England, and London.

Another famous African American scientist was Daniel Hale Williams (1856-1931). Born in Pennsylvania, Williams became a surgeon after attending university at the Chicago Medical College and opened the first interracial surgery clinic in Chicago. As an extremely accomplished surgeon, Williams became a specialist in pericardial surgery, which focuses on the heart. He made history in 1893 when he performed the first successful open heart surgery in the United States. He saved James Cornish's life, who was a patient admitted to Williams's care after a stab to the heart. Williams went on to continue his successful career in medicine, and to serve in prestigious positions on medical boards.

While the inventions and historic breakthroughs of these and other African Americans in this time period gave heart and hope to many Americans, great challenges remained. Greater equality under the law, the right to vote, the end of segregation and the start of integration, all would cohere into a Civil Rights movement that would dominate almost half of the coming century.

CHAPTER REVIEW

1. George Washington Carver was rejected from university the first time because of:
    a. his poor grades
    b. his inability to pay the fees
    c. his bad temper
    d. his race

2. George Washington Carver's work was well known and vital to scientist everywhere. Where did he become the head of the agriculture department?
    a. The United States Department of Agriculture
    b. The Congress
    c. Howard University
    d. Tuskegee Institute

3. After buying land and experimenting with plants, flowers, and agriculture, Carvers most famous discoveries or inventions?
    a. New varieties of soybeans
    b. Peanut butter
    c. Replenishing soil
    d. All of the above

4. Ernest Everett Just was most well-known for:
    a. Being the first African American to graduate from a master's program
    b. His discoveries in embryology
    c. His discovery of egg fertilization processes
    d. His discovery of peanut butter

5. Ernest Everett Just became the head of the zoology department where?
    a. The United States Department of Agriculture
    b. Dartmouth University
    c. Howard University
    d. Tuskegee Institute

6. Roger Arliner Young was a prominent:
    a. Zoologist
    b. Agriculturalist
    c. Astronomer
    d. Physicist

7. Daniel Hale Williams was the first person to do what:
    a. Eat peanut butter
    b. Operate on the heart
    c. Perform open heart surgery successfully
    d. All of the above

RECONSTRUCTION 1866 - 1900

ADDITIONAL REFERENCES ... AND FOR A "DEEPER DIVE"

Black Apollo of Science: The Life of Ernest Everett Just

By *Kenneth R. Manning*

Accomplished: African-American Women in Victorian America

By *Monroe A. Majors*

The Autobiography of an Ex-Colored Man

Reconstruction: America After the Civil War DVD

The Souls of Black Folk

By *Du Bois, W. E. B.*

Prince of Darkness: The Untold Story of Jeremiah G. Hamilton, Wall Street's First Black Millionaire

By *Shane White*

A Fragile Fragile Freedome: African American Women and Emancipation in the Antebellum

By *Dr. Erica Armstrong Dunbar*

Stony the Road: Reconstruction, White Supremacy, and the Rise of Jim Crow

By *Henry Louis Gates, Jr.*

Black Frontiers: A History of African American Heroes in the Old West

By *Lillian Schlissel*

PERIOD 5 - THE ROAD TO GREATER EQUALITY
1901-1976

CHAPTER 1

ROSA PARKS SPEAKS

The best things in life often are planned. History has painted me as some tired old woman who one day just got fed up and decided to make a scene, rather than give up my seat to a white man. In actuality, I was a Chapter Secretary of the Montgomery, Alabama branch of the NAACP. I would like to say I worked with others behind the scenes to pick the right time and place to do what I did, and pre-plan many of the nonviolent activities to follow, including the Montgomery bus boycott, but much of what happened just happened by accident, and one thing snowballed into another that winter.

That day I refused to give up my seat to a white passenger - December 1, 1955 - also wasn't the first time I clashed with that particular bus driver, James Blake. In 1933, I paid my fare in the front, then refused to get off the bus and re-enter through the back door, as our race was required to do back then. I resisted until he got so angry that he attacked me and nearly yanked off my coat sleeve. I didn't give him the satisfaction and instead left the bus. But I would remember him, he would remember me, and I think somehow we both knew this fight between us was not over.

It helps to have an education when having to deal with stubborn, ignorant people like that bus driver, and education was important to me and my family. My mother was a teacher and valued education. I attended the Alabama State Teachers' College for Negroes, in a high school "laboratory program" there, from which I got my high school degree. No question my education helped me deal with all kinds of challenges, including the institutionalized racism and inequality we faced on a daily basis.

As I said in my autobiography, "People always say that I didn't give up my seat because I was tired, but that isn't true. I was not tired physically... No, the only tired I was, was tired of giving in." All the seats in the "white" section were taken, so that same driver told those of us in the four seats of the first row of the "colored" section to stand up, to add another row to the "white" section so this white guy could sit down. The other three obeyed the driver. I refused.

Within one year, this whole thing would escalate into an almost year-long Montgomery bus boycott, with thousands of African Americans joining together to force change. On November 13, 1956, the U.S. Supreme Court ruled bus segregation was unconstitutional; the boycott ended December 20, one day after the Court's written order arrived in Montgomery.

I lost my job, but became known as "mother of the Civil Rights movement." Feels fitting that it was me, a seamstress, who wove the first thread that would string forward and become a national movement. I couldn't have been more pleased. I don't know what happened to that white bus driver.

SUMMING UP THE DECADES: 1900S TO 1960S

In the first 2/3 of the 20th century, the United States faced rapid industrialization, two World Wars, the Great Depression, the Cold War, and the Civil Rights Movement. These major events have continued to largely shape the United States and the lives of African Americans today. Violence, liberation, and struggle characterize this seventy-five year period in United States history.

The beginning of the twentieth century was marked by a period known as the Progressive Era, for the advancements made in labor laws and white women's suffrage. This period was preceded by a time in American history known as the Gilded Age, due to the lavish spending of the upper classes driven by recent advancements in technology. The main concern of the Progressive Era was, therefore, to solve the problems of the Gilded Age, by advocating for legal protections of abused workers, and eliminating problems caused by industrialization, urbanization, immigration, and political corruption. During this time, African Americans raised their own plights of rampant segregation, violence, and economic difficulties, through the writings and organizations that they established during this period.

Happening fairly simultaneously, World War I began in Europe and occurred from 1914-1918. Although the United States was only involved in World War I for its final 19 months, that involvement had enormous impacts on the history and culture of the country. When the United States declared war, African American men enlisted. At first, many were turned away because of deeply entrenched racism. Once the government realized that their current numbers of soldiers were not sufficient, four all-black regiments were put into operation and became heroes in their communities.

Then the draft came, which required men to serve in the army, and allowed African American men to join in large numbers. By the end of World War I, over 350,000 African Americans had served in the war, honorably, and with freedom in Europe that contrasted to their experiences in America. On returning home from World War I in 1919, many were fed up with poor treatment compared to overseas, which encouraged many to join organizations and continue the fight for freedom and greater legal equality and equal rights.

The 1920s also were a time of rapid spending, with the widespread use of automobiles, the spread of speakeasies defying Prohibition, and parties defining the 1920s. Prohibition was a law that banned the sale and drinking of alcohol in the United States. This period was a time of artistic revival for African American communities and came to be known - through activities primarily held in New York City - as the Harlem Renaissance. In this period, African American musicians and artists founded jazz music and were a dominant force in the artistic culture of the United States during this period.

To document and preserve this movement and the history of African Americans, Carter Godwin Woodson (1875-1950) founded a groundbreaking group titled the Association for the Study of African American Life and History (ASAALH). As the son of former slaves, Woodson became a pioneer in the study of African American history. He graduated from the University of Chicago and then Harvard University. As one of the very first scholars to ever exclusively study African American history, he is often called the "father of black history". Woodson later went on to found the *Journal of Negro History*, to foster scholarship and academic discussions around African American history. He eventually launched his idea for a black history week, which was eventually taken up as the inspiration for Black History Month, which will be explored in the 1975-present section.

Simultaneously, beginning in approximately 1916, African Americans began to migrate *en masse* out of the rural Southern United States, relocating to the Northeast, Midwest, and West. This migration, known as the Great Migration, was represented by a massive shift in African American communities northwards. For example, prior to 1910, approximately 90% of African Americans lived in the South. By the end of the Great Migration in the 1970s, 80% of African Americans either lived in the North and West or in an urban environment. In total, about six million African Americans left the South. This movement of millions of people completely reshaped the country politically and economically. The cities that they came to call home were widely impacted politically and socially by this new demographic.

The 1930s brought in the Great Depression when the stock markets crashed in 1929 due to a lack of regulation and an over pouring of reckless spending on the U.S. stock market. The 1920s had been a time of rampant consumerism backed by credit, causing an unstable market. This period was marred by some of the worst unemployment in the history of the country, with African Americans often being laid off first and hired last. As many African Americans worked in low-skilled positions such as housekeepers, they often faced the first layoffs and had little to no economic cushion. African Americans were unemployed at approximately 50% by 1932, double or triple what their white counterparts experienced.

The Great Depression finally came to an end with the beginning of World War II in Europe (1939-1945). With Adolf Hitler's takeover of Europe, the United States was drawn into World War II as a result of the bombing of Pearl Harbor. The United States joined the Allies, on the side of Great Britain and Russia, to fight the Axis, which included Germany, Italy, and Japan. The United States largely fought in Southern Europe, also known as the European Theatre, and in the Pacific Ocean, also known as the Pacific Theatre.

When African Americans joined the war effort, they still faced discrimination due to segregated units and second-class treatment at military parades, in transportation, training, and in canteens. However, African American women fought successfully to be included as nurses, with the first nurse enlisting into the Navy Nurse Corps in 1945. There were many African American heroes who served during WWII who saved lives and helped to end the war faster. The war finally ended in 1945 with the American nuclear bombings of Hiroshima and Nagasaki.

The 1950s saw a time of relative calm, with the restoration of international peace and stability in economics. For African Americans, the Civil Rights Movement took off with renewed focus and vigor with the goal of making the country inclusive, fair, and equal. The middle class grew; white Americans saw greater access to transportation, technological advancements, and a higher standard of living.

Meanwhile, many African American communities still struggled to have access to suitable schools and safe employment.

The 1960s saw a period of the ongoing struggle for civil rights as well as the Vietnam War. The Vietnam War was fought between the opposing ideological regimes in the north and south of Vietnam, with the United States supporting the Democratic administration over the Communist regime, in order to continue their struggle with the Soviet Union during the Cold War. African American men were drafted, just as were white men, to serve during this conflict. However, Vietnam was significant because it was the first conflict where black and white soldiers were integrated into the same units. Many African Americans also took part in the anti-war protests. Although equal units and solidarity were a major gain, overall, the war distracted the goals of the Civil Rights Movement and pulled attention away from the cause of equality.

CHAPTER REVIEW

1. What marked the Gilded Age?
    a. Ineffective and political corruption with conspicuous consumption
    b. Unfettered capitalism
    c. Rapid economic growth generating vast wealth for a few
    d. All of the above

2. What was the main concern of the Progressive Era?
    a. To end slavery
    b. To solve the problems of the Gilded Age
    c. To focus on advancements in technology
    d. None of the above

3. What is true about World War I?
    a. African Americans were allowed only after learning there was a shortage of soldiers
    b. There was deeply entrenched discrimination and racism in the military
    c. 350,000 African Americans serviced
    d. All of the above

4. How many African Americans left the South during the Great Migration North for a better life?
    a. 6,000
    b. 60,00
    c. 600,000
    d. 6,000,000

5. Why did many African Americans participate in the Great Migration?
    a. Labor shortages in the North
    b. Vicious and violent racism in the South
    c. Easier methods of transportation
    d. All of the above

6. TRUE or FALSE: Vietnam was the first war where black and white soldiers fought in integrated units?
    a. True
    b. False

CHAPTER 2

RESILIENCE

To better appreciate African American resilience, it's good to zero in on the depth and level of hatred that has existed in America, and the kind of situations that African Americans faced. There are many egregious examples in American history, but one of the worst was the Tulsa race riot of 1921.

Very few incidents of American history, as late as the 20th century, have been so systematically wiped from history that some question their very existence. Such was the case of the Tulsa race riot of 1921. Researchers had been challenged by police records that have been destroyed, published news articles that had been removed from archives, and (at the time) the severing of telephone and telegraph lines to the outside world, so no one could be made aware of, or assist the African-American community, as the event was happening. Thanks to one eyewitness who lived to tell what he saw, and the work of further

researchers in years since, we now have a portrait of some of the darkest moments in African-American history beginning to a lesser extent towards the end of the 19th century and growing in intensity in the early 20th century.

The Greenwood community – the African-American neighborhood within Tulsa, Oklahoma, which was home to about 10,000 – was called Black Wall Street because of its prosperity. Black Wall Street had 600 businesses, 21 churches, 30 grocery stores, 2 movie theatres, 6 private planes, a hospital, a bank, a post office, schools, libraries, law offices, and even a bus system. Since African-Americans often could not shop in white-owned stores, the money they made often went into the African American-owned businesses in their own neighborhood. When Oklahoma got its first oil wells that wealth spread into the African-American community. African-American owned businesses thrived, as did many of the residents. Many living in Greenwood were considered to be of middle or upper-class. They owned their own residential homes and were able to provide well for their families. Greenwood was a tight-knit community where everyone supported each other, which gave them all greater access to health, education, jobs, housing, savings, and resources. Despite all this, Oklahoma at the time was a segregated state, and it's fair to say that several in the white community were threatened by and envious of the financial success within the African-American neighborhood, and in some cases, were not happy with their own lack of prosperity in comparison.

On May 31 into June 1, 1921, whites – led by an estimated 2,000 Ku Klux Klan members – decided to thoroughly destroy the Greenwood neighborhood. In one of the largest massacres of African-Americans in U.S. history, over 60% of citizens in the Greenwood neighborhood were arrested by police in 16 hours, and many of the remainders were killed or injured by rampaging mobs, which aimed to destroy everything in their paths. Overnight, almost all African-American businesses and churches were destroyed, along with many residential homes, in a systematic and successful effort to obliterate the neighborhood. The neighborhood was given little money to rebuild afterward, and never returned to the level of prosperity and success it had prior to the riot. It has been estimated that, in today's dollars, the damage done to Greenwood in that one 16-hour rampage was over $30 million.

While what happened in Greenwood was especially horrific, it was far from the only incident in the 20th century. Incidents of this kind were often triggered by a false accusation, which caused white mobs already seething with hatred and jealous to unite and rally against African-Americans. Here are some other riots that preceded Tulsa, Oklahoma in the

20th century, which often were conducted against African Americans as "revenge" for their success and prosperity:

- 1906 – Little Rock, Arkansas, and Atlanta, Georgia
- 1907 – Bellingham, Washington
- 1908 – Springfield, Illinois
- 1910 – Slocum, Texas
- 1917 – East St. Louis, Illinois; Chester, Pennsylvania; and Philadelphia, Pennsylvania
- 1919 – The Red Summer of 1919 saw riots in various locations across the U.S. when white soldiers returning from World War I found in several cases that their jobs had been taken by African-American veterans.

Similar riots against African Americans followed Tulsa, before the start of the Civil Rights movement:

- 1923 - Rosewood, Florida
- 1927 – Little Rock, Arkansas
- 1927 – Poughkeepsie, New York
- 1930 – Watsonville, California
- 1935 – Harlem, Manhattan, New York
- 1943 – Detroit, Michigan; Los Angeles, California; and Harlem, Manhattan, New York (again)

While it is shocking to see this ongoing cycle of violence, it is important to recognize and acknowledge it when exploring American history in general, and African American history in particular. Individually and collectively, these riots set back the African American community – whether through people being killed or injured, or businesses or churches being destroyed or damaged. Moreover, this cycle didn't just happen in the 20th century.

THE HAMBURG RIOT, JULY, 1876

This cycle was *preceded* with riots in the 1700s and 1800s and followed with *additional* ones in the 1900s and 2000s. This continuous thread of intolerance and violence has shaped our history and our nation, and to a large extent, was successful – by bringing down the African American community and its spirit. Because later generations weren't taught or didn't know this history of assault and attack, they couldn't appreciate the struggle of their ancestors and how they had to frequently restart and rebuild, as part of living in America. Lasting poverty and despair, without fully understanding this past history of destruction and recovery, remains the lingering after-effect.

Estimates are that African American established anywhere from eighty eight to two hundred black incorporated towns throughout the United States during the 19th and early 20th centuries. These towns were all or mostly self-governing, having their own independent governments and commercial economies. The African Americans were looking for not only political freedom but economic opportunities. As it became increasing difficult to secure land in the post Confederate states, so like many whites, the African Americans sought a better life and greater opportunity in the West. The Twin Territories in Oklahoma became the most important black town centers in the nation, as thirty-two all-black towns emerged in this territory.

A list of towns founded by African American by state, not all are listed;

Alabama: Cedarlake; Greenwood Village, Hobson City, Plateau, Shepherdsville; **Arkansas**; *Edmondson, Thomasville;* **California**, *Abila, Allensworth, Bowles, Victorville;* **Colorado**; *Dearfield,* **Florida**;

Eastonville, New Monrovia, Richmond Heights, **Illnois**; *Brooklyn, Robbins,* **Iowa**; *Buxton,* **Kansas**; *Nicodmus,* **Kentucky**; *New Zion,* **Louisiana**; *Grambling North Shreveport,* **Maryland**; *Fairmont Heights, Glenarden, Lincoln City,* **Michigan**; *Idlewind, Marlborough,* **Mississippi**; *Expose, Mound Bayou, Renova,* **Missouri**; *Kinloch,* **New Jersey**; *Gouldtown, Lawnside, Springtown, Whitesboro,* **New Mexico**; *Blackdom,* **North Carolina**; *Columbia Heights, Method, Oberlin:* **Ohio**; *Lincoln Heights, Urbancrest,* **Oklahoma**; *Arkansas Colored, Bailey, Boley, Booktee, Canadian Colored, Chase, Clearview, Ferguson, Forman Gibson Station, Grayson, Langston City, Louisville, Liberty, Lima, Lincoln City, Mantu, Marshalltown, North Folk Colored, Overton, Porter, Redbird, Rentiesville, Summit, Taft, Tatum, Tullahassee, Vernon, Wellston Colony, Wybark, Two unnamed towns in Seminole Nation,* **Tennessee**; *Hortense; New Bedford, Texas, Andy Board House, Booker, Independence Heights, Kendleton, Mill City, Oldham, Roberts, Union City,* **Virginia**; *Ocean Grove Titustown, Truxton,* **West Virginia**; *Institute.*

At the same time, this cycle of violence also strengthened the determination of many individuals to contribute what they could, to try to bring it to an end.

In response to the flagrant inequality that they still experienced in nearly every facet of their lives, African Americans began to campaign for their own equality in the eyes of the law. Philosophical movements flourished during this period, and Civil Rights activists began to train and prepare for the ensuing decades of struggle. There were many areas that became focal points for the Civil Rights Movement, such as integrating schools and transportation systems, stopping lynchings, and securing fair housing, as well as making voting accessible. African American leaders founded the National Association for the Advancement of Colored People

(NAACP) to consolidate their focus.

Early on in the movement, desegregating school systems received attention because civil rights leaders wanted to provide greater equal opportunity for black children. In a landmark case in 1954, named *Brown V. Board of Education,* black students had begun a protest to call attention to their overcrowded and failing schools. This led to the NAACP filing five different court cases challenging the Jim Crow laws, a systematic legal basis for segregating and discriminating against African Americans. In 1954, the Supreme Court ruled on behalf of the NACCP, ruling that segregating schools violated the constitutional rights of the students. Therefore, in 1957, nine brave students from Little Rock, Arkansas, enrolled in a white school. They were harassed by angry whites, denied by the governor, and even had the state National Guard called to bar them access to their right. In the end, the Little Rock Nine, as they came to be called, were the first students to integrate into a white school. To do so, President Eisenhower was forced to call in the Federal National Guard to escort the students inside and out, each day. These nine students led the way for the integration of others.

The year before, Rosa Parks, a brave and strategic activist, boarded a bus, refusing to give up her seat for a white passenger in Montgomery, Alabama. In response, the black community boycotted the bus system, in what

became known as the Montgomery Bus Boycott. This boycott paved the way for the Freedom Rides in 1961, which were journeys undertaken by Civil Rights activists who traveled in buses in between Southern and Northern states to verify their right to desegregated travel between states. Often, when these travelers would step off of their buses in search of food or restrooms, they encountered extreme violence. For example, in Birmingham, Alabama, the white terrorist organization named the Ku Klux Klan (KKK) attacked the Freedom Riders. The riders were severely beaten as police often refused to protect blacks. This story repeated itself for nearly each freedom ride occurring around the country, as protesters were beaten, arrested, and attacked. Black and many whites joined to show their support against the violence. Their efforts did succeed, however, when President John F. Kennedy issued a desegregation order for buses, and by 1961, passengers were allowed to sit wherever they chose on buses.

Civil Rights activists were trained in nonviolence, the primary method Dr. King employed and encouraged, where protesters refused to fight back and use violence, even when they were beaten, imprisoned, or killed. As one example, many activists traveled to the South to further test and eliminate segregation. Many of these groups would stage sit-ins, where they would sit at counters and tables reserved for whites. These groups would dress professionally, and were instructed to sit quietly and respectfully. In response, police and white mobs would attack those sitting-in, and arrest or beat them. Non-violence demanded that these protesters bear all of the physical, emotional, and verbal abuse, and even arrest, without complaint or returning any of the violence. In spite of this brutality, their methods eventually worked, leading to desegregation in parks, theatres, museums, and beaches.

After a series of ongoing protests, marches, and riots, Dr. King journeyed to Selma, Alabama in 1963. In Selma, Dr. King and his fellow activists planned to march to the capital to demonstrate their desire for equality. Nearly six blocks into the march, local authorities, state troopers, and a white mob attacked the peaceful marchers with clubs, tear gas, barbed wire, and more. Many of the marchers were hospitalized and arrested. The evening of the second march, a white reverend who had traveled to Selma in solidarity with the marchers was attacked by white supremacists and died from his wounds. This demonstration of brutality horrified the country, and President Lyndon B. Johnson was compelled to respond.

Not all African Americans signed on to the non-violence approach, however. New and fresh voices, and approaches were added to these struggles, with the founding of the Black Power movement. Huey Newton (1942-1989) and Bobby Seale (1936) co-founded the Black Panther party to fight for the right of self-defense of African Americans as well as to foster social programs, such as the Free Breakfast for Children Programs and community health clinics. Newton and Seale learned about and experienced the ongoing struggle of African Americans, in particular in encounters with police and in poverty, and fought to create their own form of governance and self-protection.

Nevertheless, indisputable progress came. With Dr. King and his nonviolence approach on the one hand, and Malcolm X and others advocating violence on the other hand, Johnson and King worked together behind the scenes to bring the violent confrontations between Americans to a close, and help ensure that good, solid Civil Rights legislation finally would become part of the American tapestry.

On July 2, 1964, President Johnson signed into law the Civil Rights Act of 1964, which "is a landmark civil rights and U.S. labor law in the United States that outlaws discrimination based on race, color, religion, sex, or national origin. It prohibits the unequal application of voter registration requirements, and racial segregation in schools, employment, and public accommodations." It did not, however, guarantee the right to vote for African Americans, which Johnson promised to Dr. King that he would champion for and sign the legislation, after the 1964 Presidential election.

Johnson kept his promise. On August 6, 1965, he signed into law the Voting Rights Act of 1965, which has been called "a landmark piece of federal legislation in the United States that prohibits racial discrimination in voting" and (per the U.S Justice Department) "the most effective piece of federal civil rights legislation ever enacted in the country."

CHAPTER REVIEW

1. How many race riots against blacks were there between 1906 and 1943, where homes and property were destroyed and innocent people were killed?
    a. Three
    b. None
    c. More than ten
    d. Eight

2. What was the ruling of *Brown V. Board of Education*?
    a. That segregating bus system was unconstitutional
    b. That the Jim Crow laws were unconstitutional
    c. That segregating school system was unconstitutional
    d. All of the above

3. What was life like for blacks and whites during segregation?
    a. They knew very little about one another and therefore had little respect for each other
    b. They focused on each other's differences
    c. There was a great deal of hate and violence
    d. All of the above

4. Why was there a need for the NAACP?
    a. There was flagrant inequality
    b. Lynching was a common practice
    c. Voting was not allowed or inaccessible to blacks and poor whites
    d. All of the above

5. What did the freedom riders seek to accomplish?
    a. The desegregation of schools
    b. The desegregation of public transportation
    c. More involvement of African Americans in politics
    d. The abolition of the Jim Crow Laws

6. Why were the Jim Crow Laws put into place?
    a. To provide a legal and systematic methods by which to discriminate and segregate against African Americans
    b. To replace the Black Codes
    c. To provide equality for African Americans
    d. To aid African Americans during the draft

7. What did the violence at Selma against civil rights activists lead to?
    a. The passage of the Voting Rights Act of 1965
    b. The desegregation of schools
    c. The desegregation of transportation
    d. Protection for discrimination in the workplace against African Americans

8. What is the estimated number of towns established and governed by African Americans during the 19th and 20th Centuries?
    a. Four or Five
    b. Over a thousand
    c. Eighty eight to more than two hundred, not including municipalities.
    d. None

… THE ROAD TO GREATER EQUALITY 1901 - 1976

CHAPTER 3

HEROISM

When thinking of African American heroism in the early 20th century, the Tuskegee Airmen are often among the first group to come to mind. They were the first African American aviators in the U.S. Army Air Corps (AAC), a precursor of the U.S. Air Force. Trained at Tuskegee Army Air Field in Alabama, they flew more than 15,000 individual sorties in Europe and North Africa during World War II. They earned over 150 Distinguished Flying Crosses and helped encourage the eventual integration of the U.S. Armed Forces.

The Triple Nickle 555th Parachute Infantry was the nation's first all-black parachute infantry platoon, company, and battalion. They served in more airborne units in peace and war than any other parachute group in history. One of the elements in their success was that, unlike other Black infantry units officered by Whites, they were entirely Black, including the commanding officer.

In 1945, they were assigned away from combat in Europe, partly due to racism and fears that these highly trained black paratroopers wouldn't mix well with elements in Europe and could be targeted, secondly, the Japanese were bloated explosives with the intent to ignite mass fires in the forest throughout the Northwestern United States.

Heroism by African Americans took many forms in the first 2/3 of the 20th century, not only by group but by individual achievement. Ida B. Wells (1862-1931) was an investigative journalist, a leader in the Civil Rights Movement, and an educator who also helped to found the NAACP. Wells was born into slavery in Mississippi and was freed by the Emancipation Proclamation. She was orphaned early on but went to work to support her grandmother and her siblings. She went on to work as a teacher, and then became a co-owner of *The Memphis Speech and Headlight.* Through this newspaper, she began to document the ongoing lynchings in the United States and published many articles exposing lynching for the barbarous and horrific violence it was. Because of her writings, she was subject to many threats and had her newspaper attacked by a white mob. She eventually moved to Chicago, where she became very involved with the Women's Suffrage movement, as well as the Civil Rights movement. Today, Wells is remembered as a strong advocate for African Americans and for justice.

Then there is the extraordinary life of Josephine Baker (1906-1975). Baker was born in Missouri to parents who were entertainers. Baker became a celebrated entertainer, activist, and dancer. Her costumes were world-famous for their risqué nature and uniqueness. Baker originally traveled to France for her dancing career, where she was received with acclaim. However, when Germany invaded France, she assisted the Resistance by furnishing those fleeing with visas, gathering information and passing it along to the Allies, and using her job as an entertainer to gather insight into the many different countries entangled in the war. She received the Croix de Guerre by the French military for her incredible service as a spy for the French resistance. In the United States, she continued her activism, as Baker refused to perform for segregated audiences.

Henry Johnson received the Medal of Honor posthumously for his service during WWI. Johnson was born in North Carolina and joined the all-black National Guard in New York City. He was eventually sent to France, where he was put on patrol in the Argonne Forest. It was there in 1918 that the fought off a German raid in hand-to-hand combat. He sustained twenty-one wounds but saved the lives of countless fellow soldiers. For his service, he was recognized by France and was the first U.S. soldier to receive the Croix de Guerre in WWI. He overcame the racism of the army and served nobly.

Bessie Coleman (1892-1926) was another ground-breaking African American: the first African American woman to hold a pilot license, which she earned in 1921. Her early interest in flight guided her through studying in segregated schools before she moved to France to become a licensed pilot since African Americans were not allowed to become pilots in the U.S. at that time. Her dream was to open a school for African American pilots but tragically died in a plane crash.

In terms of ideology, there were many voices that described how African Americans could find liberation. One such example, is Marcus Mosiah Garvey (1887-1940), a Jamaican-born political leader and writer. Early on, he moved to the United States and became a strong voice for black political organizing when he founded the Universal Negro Improvement Association (UNIA). The UNIA aimed to found a black nation in Africa and believed in racial pride, economic self-sufficiency, and racial separation. Garvey's ideas were somewhat contentious, but they did lead to consolidation of black political power, especially for urban and poor communities.

His belief in the importance of black pride was the foundation for the idea of Pan-Africanism, which sought to unite all of the indigenous communities of Africa into a cultural and political utopia. Garvey and his followers created the pan-African flag (shown above) in response to a violently racist song declaring that African Americans had no flag. The pan-African flag is comprised of red, black, and green stripes, representing the blood of liberty, the color of the "noble and distinguished race" of African Americans, and the color of the "luxuriant vegetation of our Motherland." The flag became a symbol of Black pride and worldwide liberation.

Justice Thurgood Marshall (1908-1993) was the first African American judge on the U.S. Supreme Court. Marshall was born in Baltimore, was the descendant of slaves, yet went on to attend Howard's law school. He became a lawyer, where he argued several essential cases before the U.S. Supreme Court, such as *Brown v. Board of Education*. He also served as the Executive Director of the NAACP Legal Defense and Educational Fund. In 1961, President Kennedy appointed Marshall to the Second Circuit Court of Appeals. Four years later, President Johnson appointed him to the U.S. Supreme Court. Justice Marshall served for 24 years on the bench. He fought against the death penalty and other possible forms of unfair treatment. He also stewarded many clerkships who went on to become famous judges themselves, such as Supreme Court Justice Elena Kagan.

This period also saw the rise of some of the greatest, and most diverse, African American heroes in American history, such as Dr. Martin Luther King, Jr., Rosa Parks, Jessie Jackson, and Malcolm X, to name a few.

In terms of societal impact, Dr. King (1929-1968) was perhaps one of the greatest Americans to ever live. He was born in Atlanta, Georgia and went on to attend a historically black college. Early on, King became very interested in the ideas of nonviolent resistance that had been used by Mohandas Gandhi to free India from British colonization in 1957. King became a Baptist minister and joined the NAACP. He supported Rosa Parks and the Montgomery bus boycotts, and because he was such a visible leader, his house was bombed. King continued to lead marches, train young African Americans in the methods of nonviolence, take part in sit-ins, and organize for the freedom of African Americans. He was arrested several times, which was a tactic of nonviolence. During his Birmingham Campaign, King hoped to "create a situation so crisis-packed that it will inevitably open the door to negotiation" by organizing nonviolent action throughout the city. During these protests, the police would often use much greater force against the protesters, from letting dangerous dogs attack children, to power-spraying protesters with fire hoses, much of which was shown on national television, to the horror, shock, and revulsion of African Americans and many whites.

King was especially gifted and well-known as a speaker, or orator. He negotiated with the Federal government, led marches, and wrote some of the most well-known speeches in American history. His "I Have a Dream" speech, given on the Washington Mall, encompassed his beliefs in nonviolence, and riveted and galvanized much of the nation. After accomplishing many of his goals, King traveled to  Memphis, Tennessee, where he gave his final, and some would say most beautiful, speech, named "I've Been to the Mountaintop." Later that night, he was assassinated by James Earl Ray, a white supremacist. Also prominent in the 1960s, but taking a different approach to societal change was Malcolm X (1925-1965). Born Malcolm Little in Omaha, Nebraska, his family moved to Wisconsin after being harassed by the KKK. However, they still encountered severe racism and violence, to the point that many believe Malcolm X's father was murdered by a white supremacist group. Although he intended to practice law, Malcolm was discouraged by his teachers from doing so, because of his race. He went on to join the Nation of Islam, which advocated for black self-reliance and freedom from white supremacy, and he changed his last name to X, to symbolize the lack of the last name from his unknown ancestors (as opposed to a name given to his family by slave owners). Malcolm began to achieve fame when he stood up for a black man being beaten by police in New York City, called the Hinton Johnson incident. In the Nation of Islam, he began speaking up for African Americans, and proposing a series of radical teachings. He felt that nonviolence was too complacent a method for fighting white supremacy. He believed black communities would have to take care of themselves, solving the problems of extreme economic poverty and police brutality by defending themselves and forming their own societies. His opinions with the Nation of Islam began to diverge, and he left the organization. He was later assassinated by a member of the Nation of Islam, Talmadge Hayer, during a speech.

While discrimination faced by African Americans was bad enough, it was multiplied significantly for LGBT African Americans, who faced double discrimination for their race and their sexuality. Homosexual and transgender communities faced enormous discrimination and extra policing. In New York City, it was not uncommon for individuals to be arrested due to anti-sodomy laws, and gay nightclubs were consistently raided, which is what occurred at the Stonewall Inn, a popular gay bar, in June 1969. The night that the riots began, police raided the bar and began handcuffing and arresting LGBT patrons. In response, transgender club-goers refused to be identified, and Stormé DeLarverie, a black lesbian, cried out that someone should "Do Something." Legend has it that Marsha P. Johnson (1945-1992) threw a shot glass at a mirror and declared "I got my civil rights," which may have sparked the escalation into what became known worldwide as the Stonewall Rebellion. The incidents that evening led to massive riots around New York City for several days, where members of the LGBT community demanded equal rights, better treatment, and accountability for homophobia and police violence.

CHAPTER REVIEW

1. Who was Ida B. Wells?
    a. An investigative journalist
    b. A leader in the Civil Rights Movement
    c. An educator
    d. All of the above

2. What is Ida B. Wells most known for?
    a. Documented and investigated lynching
    b. Protested transportation discrimination
    c. Boycotted racist publications
    d. All of the above

3. Josephine Baker was:
    a. An entertainer
    b. A resistance fighter
    c. A dancer
    d. All of the above

4. Henry Johnson was a hero because he:
    a. Was a member of the French resistance
    b. Was a successful spy during WWII
    c. Fought off a German attack using hand-to-hand combat
    d. All of the above

5. What was Dr. Martin Luther King Jr's major contribution to the Civil Rights Movement?
    a. His development of the ideals of nonviolent protest
    b. His relationships with Washington politicians
    c. His willingness to be arrested
    d. His legal degree

6. Which speech encompassed Dr. King's ideology for freeing African Americans?
    a. "I've Been to the Mountaintop."
    b. "I Have a Dream"
    c. "The Ballot or the Bullet"
    d. "Native Son"

7. Malcolm X was a prominent member of which organization?
    a. The NAACP
    b. The American Bar Association
    c. The Nation of Islam
    d. All of the above

8. TRUE or FALSE: Both Martin Luther King Jr. and Malcolm X died by assassination.
    a. True
    b. False

THE ROAD TO GREATER EQUALITY 1901 - 1976

CHAPTER 4

ART

The 1910s-1930s were a golden age of African American art, known as the Harlem Renaissance. Named after the borough of New York City where the art movement began, the Harlem Renaissance was an outpouring and an explosion of black music, theatre, sculpture, painting, and more. Many artists had arrived during the Great Migration. They shattered stereotypes, explored complex themes, and celebrated blackness.

There were many prominent painters in the Harlem Renaissance who founded new forms of painting and new styles. One such artist was Aaron Douglas (1899-1979) who focused on cultivating the concept of the "New Negro." Douglas is most well-known for his mural on the New York Public Library in Harlem, which tells the story of African Americans in the United States from their ancestors in African contexts, to enslavement, to the Civil War, and finally adjusting to freedom in New York City.

Similarly, Lois Mailous Jones (1905-1998) achieved international acclaim for her paintings. Jones trained at the Boston Museum of Fine Arts but consistently lived abroad. She was often inspired by the Caribbean and African cultures for the subject matter and styles of her paintings. For example, in her painting, *Les Fetiches* (above), she used African masks to create an abstract but beautiful work.

Building off similar themes, painter Jacob Lawrence built a name for himself due to his depictions of African American everyday life. He first reached artistic acclaim for his sixty-panel painting on the Great Migration, titled *Migration Series*. This depiction of the many different aspects of the journey from the South to the North was one of the most iconic and beautiful depictions of this pivotal event. The series captured the complexity of the experiences that these travelers faced in their journeys. Each painting's name tells its historical story. In these paintings, Lawrence developed his style of "expressive cubism." Today, his paintings are spread throughout the United States, in some of the nation's most prestigious museums.

Augusta Savage was another prominent African American sculptor who made her name during the Harlem Renaissance. During the Great Depression, she was a member of a group of artists who traveled and taught artistic skills to young students. She achieved fame when she sculpted W.E.B. DuBois and Marcus Garvey. As she became more well-known, Savage was commissioned to create a sculpture for the World Fair in 1939.

CHAPTER REVIEW

1. What was the Harlem Renaissance?
    a. An explosion of artistic creativity
    b. A movement that began in New York City
    c. A literary and theatric period of expression
    d. All of the above

2. The artists of the Harlem Renaissance:
    a. Explored complex themes
    b. Celebrated blackness.
    c. Shattered stereotypes
    d. All of the Above

3. Aaron Douglas's most famous piece is:
    a. A mural at the New York Public Library
    b. *Les Fetiches*
    c. *Migration Series*
    d. "Strange Fruit"

4. Lois Mailous Jones's most famous piece is:
    a. A mural at the New York Public Library
    b. *Les Fetiches*
    c. *Migration Series*
    d. "Strange Fruit"

5. Jacob Lawrence's most famous piece is:
    a. A mural at the New York Public Library
    b. *Les Fetiches*
    c. *Migration Series*
    d. "Strange Fruit"

6. Augusta Savage achieved fame when she sculpted:
    a. W.E.B. DuBois and Marcus Garvey
    b. Prominent leaders of the Civil Rights Movement
    c. Her fellow Harlem Renaissance artists
    d. Billie Holiday

THE ROAD TO GREATER EQUALITY 1901 - 1976

CHAPTER 5

LITERATURE AND MUSIC

The Harlem Renaissance and the Civil Rights Movement also fostered enormous outpourings of literary talent. This period of literature is one of the golden ages of writing in the United States, as authors told intimate, unique, and bold stories about their lives and the lives of African Americans, at the turn of the century and beyond.

As a seminal figure in the Harlem Renaissance, Claude McKay (1889-1948) was a prominent writer and poet. His four novels - *Home to Harlem, Banjo, Banana Bottom*, and *Amiable with Big Teeth* - each made waves when they came out.

McKay was born in Jamaica but attended the Tuskegee Institute before he moved to New York, where he would spend the rest of his life. He identified with the Communist Party and was an active member of the Industrial Workers of the World before founding the influential and secret society, the African Blood Brotherhood. *Home to Harlem* won the Harmon Gold Award for Literature for his depiction of Harlem as a vivacious and complex space. This work has continued to attract international audiences for decades.

Langston Hughes (1902-1967) was one of the most breathtaking early poets of the Harlem Renaissance. He was born in Missouri but eventually moved to New York City. As a young man, Hughes was hired to work as a crewman aboard the S.S. *Malone*, where he spent six months traveling the world. He published his first poem, "The Negro Speaks of Rivers," in *The Crisis*, in association with the NAACP. His poetry electrified audiences as he spoke of the multifaceted and complex experience of African Americans. He rejected black self-hatred and contributed to the cultural nationalism of African American communities. He also wrote novels, such as *Not Without Laughter*, which won the Harmon Gold Medal for literature. Hughes is remembered for his writings, as well as for inventing a new art form, called jazz poetry.

As one of Hughes finest contemporaries, Zora Neale Hurston (1891-1960) was an equally talented writer. Hurston was born in Alabama but relocated to Florida. She used her hometown of Eatonville, Florida as the backdrop of many of her stories in the future. Hurston went to Howard University and studied anthropology while founding many societies and conducting research with some of the most well-known anthropologists of the time. She was immediately a star in New York and immersed herself in the company of Langston Hughes and Wallace Thurman. Hurston traveled extensively, studying folklore and voodoo in the Caribbean and Central America. She published her anthropological work, as well as three novels. *Their Eyes Were Watching God* was perhaps her most impactful and masterful work, as it told the intimate life story of a young African American woman in the South. Hurston was one of the most successful and detailed black female writers of the period.

 Perhaps one of the most prolific African American novelists, playwrights, poets, and activists, James Baldwin (1924-1987) made his mark on the literary culture of the United States in the period following the Harlem Renaissance. Baldwin was born in New York City and faced many obstacles in his childhood, as his father and his stepfather both died before Baldwin was twenty years old. By the time he was twenty-four, he was completely disillusioned about race relations in the country, after experiencing racist abuse from the police and in public. He moved to Paris, France, and became deeply involved in the cultural scene of France at the time. Baldwin felt particularly targeted as he was also identified as a homosexual. Baldwin's literary achievements have made their mark on literature internationally. His first novel, *Go Tell It on the Mountain*, is a semi-autobiographical account of Harlem during the 1950s. His first collection of essays, *Notes of a Native Son* became one of the most important protest novels in American history. His second novel, *Giovanni's Room*, was one of the first works to be published openly telling the moving and deeply thoughtful story of an interracial gay romance. His writings, paired with his activism (in one interview, he called the Statue of Liberty "nothing but a bitter joke"), render Baldwin one of the more controversial, and memorable, figures in American history.

Along with authorship, African-Americans started to make noticeable headway in publishing ventures. John H. Robinson debuted *Ebony Magazine* in 1945, vowing to showcase the happier side of African-American life, as well as *Jet Magazine*. *Ebony* reported on that happier side with success stories but also covered ongoing racism. In 1955, *Jet Magazine* published a graphic photograph of the 14-year-old murdered boy, Emmett Till, in his coffin, at the request of his mother, to "show the world what they had done to my son." John H. Robinson was the grandson of slaves and was the first African-American to be published on the Forbes List of the 400 Richest Americans.

Musicians also experienced a renaissance during this period, with the popularization of jazz music. One of the most important of these musicians was Billie Holiday. Her incredible voice inspired jazz musicians and led to the pioneering of tempo, in part because she had a knack for improvisation. Although Holiday never received any formal musical education, she began singing in Harlem nightclubs and was eventually signed onto a recording contract. She is perhaps most well-known for her performance of "Strange Fruit," a song describing the horrors of lynching.

But in terms of national and worldwide impact, the invention of Motown music by Berry Gordy, Jr. not only revolutionized American music by creating a new genre, but played an important social role in breaking down the barriers of segregation, and enabling integration in performing venues and on national television. As producer and promoter, Berry Gordy, Jr. made it possible for hundreds of African American singers and entertainers to have a huge positive impact on the world.

Martha Reeves (of Martha and the Vandellas, singer of "Heat Wave," "Dancing in the Streets," and other hit songs) recalled in her autobiography how, when they only wanted to go to the bathroom, they faced a man with a double-barreled shotgun in the South, in the fittingly named town of Lynchburg, Mississippi. In Memphis, Tennessee one month later, on December 1, 1962, one side of the audience "white only," the other side "black only," they were instructed to "sing each song twice, first facing white, then facing black." No wonder we needed a Civil Rights Act.

Yet, one after another, the Motown machine kept producing hit songs, singers, and groups, making American history and changing American culture. Although the Motown artists were hugely talented in their own right, the worldwide popularity of the Beatles in 1964 helped in a small way to popularize Motown music throughout the world, especially when they performed on the same bill with African American artists in formerly "white only" concert venues. The Beatles covered Motown songs on their first album, and Motown returned the favor a few years later when multiple Motown artists covered Beatles songs. The Beatles said they were entranced by Motown music, and their albums clearly show its influence on their artistry.

Breaking the color barrier also happened on national television. Popular shows like The Ed Sullivan Show always led the national conversation with who they aired, so it became a big deal when the Supremes and other African American singers appeared on various segments of his show in the 1960s and 1970s. The Supremes appeared on The Ed Sullivan Show a whopping 17 Sundays in total. African Americans on television were no longer just slaves, comedy foils, servants, or the working-class. They were international stars.

Important breakthroughs would continue on television through the 1960s and 1970s. In 1963 on CBS, Cicely Tyson became the first African American woman to appear as a series regular on a national primetime dramatic TV series, "East Side/West Side." In 1968, Diahann Carroll starred in "Julia," the first African American star of her own series who was not portraying a domestic worker. Norman Lear's TV series brought several more breakthroughs, from the first interracial kiss on national television between two men - Carroll O'Connor as Archie Bunker, and Sammy Davis, Jr, on "All in the Family" in 1972 - and in 1975, the first African American interracial couple in a TV-series cast in "The Jeffersons" with actors Franklin Cover (Caucasian) and Roxie Roker (African American) as Tom and Helen Willis, respectively.

CHAPTER REVIEW

1. TRUE or FALSE: The Harlem Renaissance also included literature.
    a. True
    b. False

2. Langston Hughes is most well-known for his:
    a. Novels
    b. Poetry
    c. Journalism
    d. Auto-biographies

3. Langston Hughes wrote which of the following:
    a. "The Negro Speaks of Rivers"
    b. *Their Eyes Were Watching God*
    c. *Giovanni's Room*
    d. *Go Tell It On The Mountain*

4. Which state did Zora Neale Hurston often use as the backdrop for her stories?
    a. New York
    b. Alabama
    c. Missouri
    d. Florida

5. Zora Neale Hurston wrote which of the following:
    a. "The Negro Speaks of Rivers"
    b. *Their Eyes Were Watching God*
    c. *Giovanni's Room*
    d. *Go Tell It On The Mountain*

6. Baldwin felt extremely ostracized because he was:
    a. African American
    b. Gay
    c. Poor
    d. All of the above

7. Baldwin wrote which of the following?
    a. *Giovanni's Room*
    b. "Native Son"
    c. *Go Tell It On The Mountain*
    d. All of the above

CHAPTER 6

SPORTS

This period was also a golden age for African Americans entering sports, who broke open doors and the color barrier and showing their skill and talent in a wide variety of sports. Track and field, basketball, boxing, and rodeo all saw African American athletes at the top of their game in this time period.

Figure 1. George Poage in 1903.
(Courtesy Murphy Library, UW-La Crosse)

For example, George Poage (1880-1962) was born in Wisconsin, was the salutatorian of his high school class, and went on to compete in track in college at the University of Wisconsin. He was famous for his performance in track and field in the 1904 Olympics, winning two medals.

Poage's legacy was carried forward by Jesse Owens (1913-1980), who won four gold medals at the 1936 Olympic Games in Berlin and held the long jump record for nearly three decades. Owens was born in Alabama and was recognized for his incredible speed early on when he won three track events in high school. Owens was called the "The Buckeye Bullet" because of his unbelievable speed, as he broke four world records before even qualifying for the Olympics. His performance in the Olympics flew in the face of the violent racism preached by Adolf Hitler, who had criticized U.S. officials for allowing the inclusion of African Americans in the Olympics. For his performance, he was later rewarded with the Presidential Medal of Freedom by President Gerald Ford.

Ora Mae Washington (1898-1971) born in Carolina County Virginia was the first prominent African American athlete to dominate two sports, tennis and basketball. She won her first national tournament in 1925, and her first national championship within a year of picking up the racket. Tennis as a sport was racially segregated so her opponents were other African Americans. In response to the USTA ban on black players competing in their tournaments, a group of African American businessmen, college professors, and physicians founded the American Tennis Association (ATA) in Washington D.C. on November 30, 1916. The ATA is the oldest black sports organization in the United States.

Then there is "The Great One," the one and only Muhammed Ali, born Cassius Clay (1942-2016). Born in Kentucky, Ali began training as an amateur boxer from a young age. By age 18, he had already won a gold medal at the 1960 Summer Olympics. Ali achieved fame when he won a major upset victory against the heavyweight championship from Sonny Liston. Ali is the only three-time champion of the heavyweight boxing division, as he defeated dozens of challengers. Ali is well-known for more than just his unparalleled boxing ability, but also for his activism, as he joined the Nation of Islam. His participation in the Nation of Islam caused him to change his name. Ali refused the Vietnam draft and fought for equality for African Americans. He loved the spotlight and brought a level of confidence and power to his performance unseen before. Ali is widely regarded as the most significant sportsman of the twentieth century and later went on to be a public face for Parkinson's disease, as well as a raiser of awareness and funds for charitable causes around the world.

Muhammed Ali was far from the only great African American boxer. The list of ESPN's Best Boxers of All Time includes several African American men: Ali; Sugar Ray Robinson; Floyd Maywether, Jr.; Joe Louis; Mike Tyson; Lennox Lewis; Evander Holyfield; and Manny Pacquiano.

In the sport of basketball, an incredible team was formed, named The Harlem Globetrotters, which combined basketball with visual theatrics. This group combined sport and theatre by holding performance games. They participated in the World Professional Basketball Tournament and won in 1940. Just eight years later, they again beat one of the most well-known white basketball teams in the country, the Minneapolis Lakers. They still perform today around the world.

Finally, the Southwestern Colored Cowboys Association (SCAA) formed in the late 1940s, by black cowboys, to allow African Americans to compete in rodeo events. The SCAA sponsored "All Colored" rodeo events, particularly in Oklahoma and Texas, building on the "Soul Circuit" minority rodeos in the Texas Gulf region. While the Professional Rodeo Cowboys Association (PRCA) was created in 1936 to sanction official rodeo events, and never officially barred African Americans from competing in its events, Jim Crow, segregation, and other laws and racial attitudes did prevent African American cowboys from competing in white-sponsored rodeos. In 1966, Myrtis Dightman broke the color barrier and became the first African American cowboy in the SCAA to qualify for the PRCA National Finals Rodeo; while in 1982, Charlie Sampson became the first African American to win in the PRCA National Finals.

THE ROAD TO GREATER EQUALITY 1901 - 1976

CHAPTER REVIEW

1. For which sport was George Poage known?
    a. Boxing
    b. Basketball
    c. Track and Field
    d. Golf

2. George Poage is well-known because:
    a. He broke four world records before he was 18
    b. He was a prominent activist and athlete
    c. He was considered the greatest runner of all time
    d. He was the first African American to compete in the Olympic Games

3. For which sport was Jesse Owens known?
    a. Boxing
    b. Basketball
    c. Track and Field
    d. Golf

4. Jesse Owens achieved acclaim because:
    a. He won gold medals at the Berlin Olympics
    b. He broke four world records early on
    c. His attendance of the Olympics in spite of Adolf Hitler discouraging the participation of African Americans
    d. All of the above

5. For which sport was Muhammed Ali known?
    a. Boxing
    b. Basketball
    c. Track and Field
    d. Golf

6. Ali participated in which organization:
    a. The Sportsman's League of America
    b. The Nation of Islam
    c. The NAACP
    d. All of the above

CHAPTER 7

MATH AND SCIENCE

African Americans also entered the scientific and mathematical fields in force. Chemistry, astrophysics, engineering, and more all benefited immensely from the talents of African Americans. As these fields experienced enormous change during the twentieth century, African Americans helped to bring science forward. There were also horrendous moments wherein African Americans were targeted for experiments undertaken by white scientists. One terrible example of this is the Tuskegee Study of Untreated Syphilis.

This experiment was conducted between (1932-1972) by the U.S. Public Health Service, which worked with the Tuskegee Institute to observe untreated syphilis in African American men. The men recruited for the study were poor sharecroppers. Of the participants, a portion of them had never had the disease, and unbeknownst to them, they were deliberately infected with the deadly illness. Although the study was only supposed to last for six months, it actually dragged on for forty years. When the study lost funding, the scientists working on it never informed the participants that they had syphilis, which was entirely treatable by penicillin. They refused treatment to these participants, and never gave them the full disclosure of the study. As a result, many died - along with their wives, who also contracted the disease, and their children, who were born with congenital syphilis. This study has been named the most controversial and horrifying biomedical study in U.S. History and led to the 1979 Belmont Report as well as the Institutional Review Boards for the protection of research subjects.

On a more positive note, there are many examples of African American excellence in science during this period. One example is Percy Lavon Julian (1899-1975), who was a noted chemist who helped to standardize critical medications, such as steroids, birth control, and more. Julian was the valedictorian of his class and went on to attend DePauw University before moving on to Harvard for graduate school. He went abroad to receive his Ph.D. before returning home to teach at Howard University. He made serious advances in understanding and synthesizing hormones from plants. His methods also helped to develop new technologies for treating rheumatoid arthritis as well as ground-breaking birth control drugs. Julian was later elected to the National Academy of Sciences for his achievements.

Garrett Augustus Morgan, Sr. (1877-1963) was born to former slaves and educated to a sixth-grade level. Despite the lack of extended education, he became a prominent inventor, creating a smoke hood, the three-level traffic signal, and other public safety-related devices, as well as chemical products for straightening hair.

Katherine Johnson was a celebrated mathematician who calculated orbital mechanics by hand, leading the way in the success of the Space Shuttle program. Born in West Virginia, Johnson was extremely gifted in mathematics from an early age but was denied further education because her school district did not offer public schooling for African Americans children past the eighth grade. She went on to graduate from college with a degree in mathematics and French at age 18. Johnson successfully applied for a job at NASA as a mathematician, which became a historical precedent. Her brilliance was quickly noticed as she contributed to the ongoing projects of NASA, helping to calculate the launch window for the 1961 Mercury Mission, for Alan Shepard's 1961 space flight, and much more. Johnson made her mark on astrophysics in such a profound way that a movie, named *Hidden Figures*, was recently made to tell both the story of her life, as well as to honor her as a true pioneer in the field.

Marie Maynard Daly (1921-2003) was a striking biochemist, and the first black woman in the United States to earn a Ph.D. in Chemistry. Daly was born in New York City and attended a high school where she was encouraged to pursue chemistry. Because of the ongoing war, Daly received fellowships at New York University and Columbia to continue her education and research in chemistry. She went on to

work at Howard University, where she made significant discoveries related to nuclear proteins. Her work was also used by Watson and Crick in their descriptions of the structure of DNA. Her discoveries are considered fundamental in several fields today.

There are also essential contributions that African Americans made who were not trained as formal scientists. One of the most interesting of these cases is that of Henrietta Lacks (1920-1951). Born in Virginia, Lacks worked as a tobacco farmer from a young age and then moved to Baltimore. In exploring an illness, samples of tissue were taken from her without her knowledge, leading to a discovery of cancer. After her death from cancer, it was found that her cancer cells were discovered to contain the HeLa cell, the first immortalized cell line and one of the most groundbreaking, important cell lines in biomedicine today. Her cells have allowed for enormous leaps in medical research, have cured diseases, and have substantially changed the medical research field.

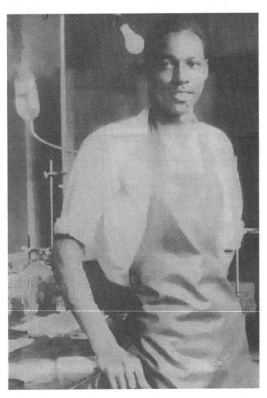

Dr. Vivien T. Thomas was the grandson of a slave and became an African-American surgical technician who pioneered procedures in the 1940s to treat "blue baby syndrome," where babies turned blue due to deprivation of oxygen. It was a complex and fatal four-part heart anomaly, which he solved by performing research and surgery on dogs, then applying that knowledge to humans. Since he never had a formal medical degree – his highest education was the completion of high school – he was never allowed to operate on a living patient, but would guide surgeons by being present with them in the operating room. He was awarded an Honorary Doctorate by Johns Hopkins University in 1976 – a Doctorate in Laws rather than a medical doctorate – and after working there for 37 years, he finally was appointed to the faculty School of Medicine as an Instructor of Surgery.

Having made huge contributions to society throughout the early 20th century - in fields including but not limited to art, literature, music, sports, math, and science - education continued to be the thread that tied together centuries of African-American achievement and progress. By 1976, African Americans were poised to celebrate the American Bicentennial - the 200th anniversary of the signing of the *Declaration of Independence*, and the founding of the United States of America - with a greater overall level of formal education, and greater freedom and equality, than they'd had at any earlier time in America. Yes, there were still problems, and challenges - poverty, crime, drugs, and mistreatment by the police - and there were still lengthy debates and discussions about the legacies of racism, slavery, and inequality, but there was noticeable progress when compared to previous centuries. African Americans had equal rights under the law. African Americans had the right to vote. African Americans had broken the color barrier in almost every field of prominence. Forced segregation had come to an end, and schools were now integrated, which gave African Americans access to higher quality education, a long-sought goal. In American politics, there were African American mayors, governors, assemblymen, members of the House of Representatives, Senators, and a hopeful belief that someday, there might even be an African American President or Vice President.

But even 200 years in, there had never been one national moment in America where pretty much *everyone* - white, African American, and beyond - was talking about the history of slavery, and the legacy and impact it still had, generations after its departure. To the surprise of many, that unanticipated national moment of conversation came one year later, in 1977.

CHAPTER REVIEW

1. Percy Lavon Julian was a noted:
    a. Astrophysicist
    b. Chemist
    c. Neuroscientist
    d. Biologist

2. Julian was prominent in his field because of his discoveries related to:
    a. Synthesizing hormones
    b. Treating rheumatoid arthritis
    c. Formulating new birth control drugs
    d. All of the above

3. Katherine Johnson was a pioneering:
    a. Mathematician
    b. Biologist
    c. Neuroscientist
    d. Chemist

4. Johnson worked on which project?
    a. Helping to calculate the launch window for the 1961 Mercury Mission
    b. Calculating a window for Alan Shepard's 1961 space flight
    c. Calculating more precise take-off procedures
    d. All of the above

5. Marie Maynard Daly was an ingenious:
    a. Mathematician
    b. Astrophysicist
    c. Biologist
    d. Chemical biologist

6. Marie Maynard Daly was the first:
    a. African American woman to work at NASA
    b. African American woman to attend Harvard
    c. African American woman to graduate university at the age of 18
    d. African American woman to earn a PhD

7. Marie Maynard Daly's findings were cited by which famous scientist(s)?
    a. Charles Darwin
    b. Edwin Hubble
    c. Watson and Crick
    d. George Washington Carver

8. With little formal education, Garrett Augustus Morgan Invented?
    a. Surgical equipment used in hospitals
    b. An automatic device used in manufacturing
    c. The three level traffic signal
    d. All of the above

9. Dr. Vivien T. Morgan pioneered procedures in what area?
    a. Brain surgery
    b. Knee surgery
    c. Heart surgery
    d. Cancer research

AFRICAN AMERICAN HISTORY

ADDITIONAL REFERENCES ... AND FOR A "DEEPER DIVE"

The Story of Tuskegee Airman
By Lynn Homan and Thomas Reilly

Our Kind of People: Inside America's Black Upper Class
By Lawrence Otis Graham Black Knight

The Divine Nine: The History of African American Fraternities and Sororities Kindle Edition
By Lawrence C. Ross

Revolution in Our Lifetime: A Short History of the Black Panther Party
By Donna Murch

Slavery By Another Name
Sam Pollard (Director)
Rated: PG
Format: DVD

I Am Not Your Negro
Samuel L. Jackson (Actor), James Baldwin (Actor), Raoul Peck (Director)
Rated: PG-13
Format: DVD

Defining Moments in Black History: Reading Between the Lies
By Dick Gregory

PERIOD 6 - THE AGE OF RECKONING 1977-2019

CHAPTER 1

A TV EXECUTIVE REFLECTS ON 1977

I was proud to be part of "must see TV." While those of us in television knew the sweep of history and the tracing of the family to Africa detailed in Alex Haley's novel *Roots* would appeal to African-Americans, we wanted to take that memorable story and get white viewers to watch, as well. To do that, we assembled a top-line African-American cast and paired them off with popular and well-liked white actors cast against type to portray slave owners and plantation masters, including Lorne Greene from *Bonanza*, Ralph Waite from *The Waltons*, and Ed Asner from *The Mary Tyler Moore Show*. The end result, to our surprise, launched a truly national, conversation on slavery and its legacy, by whites, African Americans, and others.

In 1977, over eight consecutive evenings, ABC aired "Roots: The Saga of an American Family," and the saga of one American family. From Kunta Kinte to Alex Haley, the story propelled a national conversation on race relations and a remarkable reckoning of America's past history with African Americans.

The shackles. The slave ships. The tearing apart of families at slave auctions. The sexual and physical abuse. The torture. The whippings. The bruises. For the first time in their lifetimes, a shocked America saw all of the ups and downs of African American history, replayed in graphic detail and living color.

There were also the marriages, the births, the deaths, the continuance of lives and generations, the rising to challenges, and the triumphs. Learning to read, trying to escape, doing what thousands of others did across generations, and becoming the shared threads that shape our shared history.

"Roots" was certainly not the first memorable African American story put on television. Cicely Tyson in "The Autobiography of Miss Jane Pittman" is one previous example of "must see TV," and there are hundreds of other examples.

What made "Roots" so unique was its audience, and the fact it aired over eight consecutive nights: January 23 to 30, 1977. What happened the night before in the show was what pretty much everyone who saw the show talked about the next day - in the family, in the office, at the bar, etc. That was, and is, the power of television - and for the first time, that national power was being used to address the history of slavery, in a way that had never been done before. At that time, there was no Internet, and the three networks - ABC, CBS, and NBC - still held national dominance. And dominate is what "Roots" did.

According to one Internet source, "The miniseries was watched by an estimated 130 million and 140 million viewers total (*more than half of the U.S. 1977 population of 221 million—the largest viewership ever attracted by any type of television series in U.S. history,* as tallied by Nielsen Media Research) and averaged a 44.9 rating and 66% to 80% viewer share of the audience. The final episode was watched by 100 million viewers, and an average of 80 million viewers watched each of the last seven episodes. Eighty-five percent of all television homes saw all or part of the miniseries. All episodes rank within the List of most watched television broadcasts top 100 rated TV shows of all time." Over 40 years after it first aired, the miniseries finale "still holds a record as the third-highest-rated episode for any type of television series, and the second-most watched overall series finale in U.S. television history." For a modern point of comparison, the much-touted 2019 final season opener of "Game of Thrones" had an estimated viewership of about 17.4 million.

I can't say what lasting impact the initial airing of *Roots* had. For one week, it was reported that African Americans were approached by white people in tears in some cases, or with a little more respect or courtesy - the holding open of a door, a smile of respect or acknowledgment. Again, 85% of Americans with a television watched all or part of that story. We united America, possibly in the greatest national moment of shared humanity via television since men landed on the moon in 1969.

I understand there are people in America in 2019 who claim we need to have a national conversation on race. I'd like to remind them that, for eight days and nights in 1977, we did.

SUMMING UP THE DECADES, THE 1970S TO 2010S

The 1970s to 2010s were still times of struggle for equality, but African Americans had now achieved a new status in society. They could use the tools that were won during the Civil Rights Movement to obtain admission to universities, gain employment without discrimination vote without restriction, shine a light on the crimes of racism, and begin to flourish in every sector of society more easily than had occurred in the past.

The 1970s saw several firsts of notable progress. In 1971, Walter Bremond set up Bufi, a fund that stood for his belief that African Americans "had a responsibility to assist in our growth and development, that we could not forever go to the larger white community and ask for support of programs we believe are important for our survival without doing something ourselves." If history is any example, dating back to when blacks first came to America, their accomplishment and successes had come with little aid from those outside their communities. Upward mobility in the life of the average African Americans often hinged upon long hours of hard labor, getting involved in government, and the writing and passing of laws. During the reconstruction era of 1865, and within a few years of emancipation, as many as 16 African American were elected to Congress with the hope of redressing the inequalities of slavery and its social, political and economic legacy.

With the enactment of the Jim Crow Laws -1876-1965 and North Carolina Representative George White's departure from the House of Representatives in March 1901, there were no African American who served in the U.S. Congress for nearly three decades, As of 2019, there is greater representation in some areas – 52 House members are black, putting the share of black House members (12%) on par with the share of blacks in the U.S. population. Voter suppression, however, is still very much a part of the current American system and vigilance is required to ensure access to all citizens.

Another set of policies that had a devastating impact on African American communities were Richard Nixon's "War on Drugs," which professed to deal with the cocaine and crack epidemics. But John Ehrlichman, Nixon's legal counsel, summed up Nixon's real intention of the War on Drugs very clearly,

in *Harper's Magazine* in 1994: "The Nixon White House ... had two enemies: the antiwar left and black people. Do you understand what I'm saying? We knew we couldn't make it illegal to be either against the war or blacks, but by getting the public to associate the hippies with marijuana and blacks with heroin, and then criminalizing both heavily, we could disrupt those communities. We could arrest their leaders, raid their homes, break up their meetings, and vilify them night after night on the evening news. Did we know we were lying about the drugs? Of course, we did." Today, many scholars and politicians agree that this policy more severely targeted African American communities, resulting in extremely high rates of incarceration and unfair treatment.

The failed approach continued under another name in the mid-1980s, via Nancy Reagan's "Just Say No" campaign, and remains yet another attempt to criminalize, marginalize, and continue a negative mass smear campaign against African Americans. The prison industry in American exceeds 81billion dollars a year. Many have akin this profit making industry to another method of slavery, which enriched the pockets of rich white southern at the expense of African Americans and the rest of the nation.

The 1990s brought the Clintons into office, and the country benefited from a rare Federal budget surplus, combined with a productive economy and low unemployment, as well as the first substantial discussions about a national health care plan. This brought some degree of prosperity and good feeling across the country.

The 2000s were changed forever when the United States entered the War in Iraq and Afghanistan due to the September 11th attacks on New York. Twelve African American first responders heroically gave their lives that day, and others saved lives. Regina Wilson was one such responder, as the only female firefighter in her firehouse. She acted with bravery and noted that she hoped people would see her sacrifice and the fact that African Americans also were important heroes.

The ebb and flow of progress and setbacks from the 1970s to the 2010s has led to discussions about creating a more even and equal economic and educational playing field for African Americans. Although the degree of past atrocities probably can and never will be fully addressed, it is a step in the right direction to argue that America will never heal, until the past injustices and those responsible for them – the riots, the incarcerations, the systemic racism and violence against African American communities – are brought to trial, and true justice is allowed to prevail. Justice can take many forms. Some argue that African American communities need to be the focus for stimulus packages. Other individuals – including, for the first time, several Democratic candidates for President of the United States in 2020 – have argued for "reparations" for the past violence toward African Americans, the after-effects of which still affect the African American community today. Whether they will happen, and what form such "reparations" may take, will be the subject of discussion as we enter into the 2020s, and continue and further expand on the earlier national conversations we've had.

CULTURAL ICONS

At the same time, several African-American men and women reached new heights of success – in jobs and political ventures, in business, in wealth, and in human achievement – worthy of individual note during this time period. Here are a few success stories of note between 1977 and 2019.

Oprah Winfrey is a multitalented, multifaceted African-American who rose from poverty and abuse to become a billionaire (net worth estimated at $3.5 billion). She has been an actress, producer, business entrepreneur, popular talk show host, and philanthropist. The Oprah Winfrey Show, nationally syndicated from 1986 to 2011, was among the most popular in the genre.

Tyler Perry is an American playwright, director, screenwriter, actor, and comedian, well-known for his Madea series of movie comedies. In 2011, Forbes listed him as the highest paid man in entertainment, earning $130 million between May 2010 and May 2011.

Michael Jordan regarded as the greatest basketball player of all time, winning six NBA titles, is also the owner of his own team the Hornets, worth over a billion dollars. He is also the shining star of endorsements with lucrative post-career contracts with several leading corporations.

Robert L Johnson was the founder of BET (Black Entertainment Television) and became the first African-American billionaire. He also founded RLJ Companies, which invests in several business sectors. Johnson became the first African-American majority club owner of a major American sports league with his 2002 purchase of the Charlotte Bobcats.   He has been on many Board of Directors, including the United Negro College Fund and the National Museum of African-American History and Culture and many corporate boards.

Marian Wright Edelman is Founder and President of the Children's Defense Fund, later Founder of another organization called Stand for Children, and has been an activist and advocate for disadvantaged children for all of her adult life. She was the first African-American woman to be admitted to the Mississippi Bar and helped establish the Federal Head Start program. She has been quoted as saying, "If you don't like the way the world is, you have an obligation to change it. Just do it one step at a time."

Ben Carson was a gifted neurosurgeon best known for separating conjoined twins, and later had an unsuccessful run for President of the United States. In 2017, he became the 17th United States Secretary of Housing and Urban Development.

John Lewis, a sharecropper's son, has served 17 terms in the U.S. House of Representatives since 1987 and is the Representative for Georgia's Fifth District, which includes about ¾ of the city of Atlanta. In the Civil Rights movement, he was one of the original 13 Freedom Riders in 1960; and Chairman of the Student Nonviolent Coordinating Committee (SNCC) from 1963-1966, which involved him playing a major role both in coordinating the 1963 March on Washington and speaking at it. He was the youngest speaker at that March at age 23, and the only speaker who is still alive in 2019.

Finally, in a different kind of personal achievement, Willie Duberry died in 1991 at the age of 121 years and 279 days, making him the oldest person in the world at that time, per the *Guinness Book of World Records*. Unlike other claimants, he had documented proof of his age: a 1900 U.S. Census form listing his birthday as February 7, 1870, in Summerville, South Carolina. His longevity provides lasting hope that if we too could live to 121, we might see full equality, justice, and economic prosperity in America.

CHAPTER REVIEW

1. The Post-Civil Rights US afforded African Americans the legal tools to:
    a. Gain admission to universities
    b. Gain employment without discrimination
    c. Vote without restriction
    d. All of the above

2. Which set of laws directly targeted African Americans
    a. The War on Drugs
    b. The Jim Crow Laws
    c. Just Say No Campaign
    d. All of the above

3. TRUE or FALSE: The War on Drugs was effective.
    a. True
    b. False

4. How many African American first responders lost their lives in 9/11?
    a. 1
    b. 12
    c. 50
    d. 3

5. Self-Made African American Billionaires of the 20th Century
    a. Oprah Winfrey
    b. Robert L. Johnson
    c. Michael Jordan
    d. All of the Above

6. John Lewis a sharecropper's son demonstrated bravery, resilience, intelligence and hope for a better America when he:
    a. Joined as one of the original thirteen Freedom Riders in 1960
    b. Served seventeen terms in the U.S. House of Representatives
    c. Played a major role in coordinating the March on Washington in 1963
    d. All of the above

CHAPTER 2

RESILIENCE

From the mid-1970s forward, important political and ideological movements continued to pick up steam, including the Black Power movement. This movement emphasized the importance of black excellence, economic empowerment, and the need for founding cultural institutions to foster African American history and art. The movement grew out of the Civil Rights Movement as advocates were able to engage further with political lobbying and even armed struggle to fight for their freedom. This also led to the founding of black businesses, food cooperatives, farms, media, printing presses, clinics, schools, and medical services. It was led in part by Robert F. Williams and Malcolm X, with the Black Panther Party as its cornerstone. The influence of Black Power spread throughout the world, manifesting the decolonization movements throughout many African nations and also in the Cuban Revolution.

 There were many marches and political movements that drew upon the momentum and the ideas of the Black Power movement led by Huey P. Newton and Bobby Seale. For example, the Million Man March was a massive gathering of African American men in Washington, D.C., in 1995. The March sought to convey to the world a vastly different picture of the African American male and invited many prominent speakers as well as political groups to join them. They undertook voter registration, presented teach-ins, and formulated a political agenda to address urban poverty and other issues.

One example of African American resilience is Angela Davis, an American political activist and author. She worked with the Communist Party of America to 1991, and was involved with the Black Panther Party during the Civil Rights movement, though she did not support the Million Man March, due to its male-centric focus. These days, at the University of Santa Cruz, California, she is a Distinguished Professor Emerita in the History of Consciousness Department. She also was one of the founders of Critical Resistance, a grassroots organization and movement to abolish the prison-industrial complex, which she has called a new version of slavery.

Two issues that continue to plague African American communities is the aforementioned prison-industrial complex, and police brutality. Michael Brown, a black 18-year old, was shot twelve times and killed by a white 28-year-old police officer named Darren Wilson in Ferguson, Missouri. Three months after Brown's killing, two officers shot and killed 12-year old Tamir Rice in Cleveland, Ohio. A Chicago police officer shot and killed 17-year old Laquan McDonald sixteen times in one minute, causing his death. In Maryland, 25-year old Freddie Gray was taken into custody by Baltimore police, due to the possession of an illegal knife.

While some police officers may have outright discrimination or racism toward black Americans, some psychologists and race experts believe these officers are impacted by subconscious white supremacy. This implicit bias, a deeply internalized belief that African Americans are dangerous, has affected all levels of justice in U.S. society, from the officers that commit these atrocities to the policymakers who draft laws that disproportionately affect black communities, to the juries who refuse to prosecute these officers.

These and other killings have gravely exacerbated a lack of trust between African. As many African American communities feel powerless in addressing the police on an individual scale, networks and groups, such as Black Lives Matter (BLM), have been formed as a power currency to vocalize grievances and achieve justice as a collective, and have provided a major groundswell of support to hold police accountable for excessive racism-based violence.

To be fair, there are many white police officers who are respectful when dealing with African Americans and are themselves outrage over the killings cited above. Dealing with a system entrenched in a white supremacy ideology for over two hundred years makes weeding out the bad a lonely endeavor. But on a hopeful note, better-integrated police departments, community policing, joint meetings between the police and members of the community, and the installation and use of video cameras on police officers are among the measures being introduced, and which are collectively making positive, tension-reducing effects in police/community relations when implemented comprehensively.

CHAPTER REVIEW

1. The Black Power Movement sought to:
    a. Support black businesses, food cooperatives, farms, media, printing presses, clinics, schools, and medical services.
    b. Emphasize the importance of black cultural institutions
    c. Empower African Americans
    d. All of the Above

2. Who were some of the leaders of the Black Power Movement?
    a. Robert F. Williams
    b. Malcolm X
    c. Huey Newton
    d. All of the Above

3. The Million Man March sought to:
    a. Convey to the world a vastly different picture of the Black male
    b. Protest the Vietnam War
    c. Protest the AIDS/HIV Epidemic
    d. All of the Above

4. What did the killing Michael Brown and the lack of justice cause?
    a. The founding of Black Lives Matter
    b. A national conversation about police brutality
    c. Riots in Ferguson
    d. All of the above

5. TRUE or FALSE: Police refused to give Freddie Gray medical treatment after tackling him and using excessive force during his arrest, leading to his death.
    a. True
    b. False

6. Implicit Bias can be defined as:
    a. Outright white supremacy and racism
    b. A method of police brutality
    c. A deeply internalized or subconscious belief that black Americans are dangerous
    d. A training technique to lessen racism amongst police officers

7. Black Lives Matter strives to:
    a. Achieve justice as a collective
    b. Voice grievances
    c. Abolish police brutality
    d. All of the above

CHAPTER 3

HEROISM

African Americans continued to play a significant role in every aspect of politics, culture, and the fight for a more just society. Here are some of the many.

Stokely Carmichael (1941-1998) was an early advocate for Civil Rights, Pan-Africanism, and Black Power. Born in Trinidad, Carmichael grew up in the United States from the age of eleven. After turning down a full ride scholarship to Harvard University, he went on to attend Howard University, a predominately black university, where he led the Student Nonviolent Coordinating Committee (SNCC). While there, he participated in the 1961 Freedom Rides and was arrested. He was jailed for forty-nine days and was the youngest detainee. He became a full-time organizer, coordinating with the NAACP and becoming the chairman of the SNCC. He often worked on voting rights challenges and protests. He joined the black power movement and was later seen as Malcolm X's direct successor. Because of this and his impressive work, he was directly targeted by the FBI. Carmichael fled to Ghana and then Guinea and adopted a new name: Kwame Ture.

Jesse Jackson also represented this massive shift for new power and political incorporation, as he became the first African American to receive Presidential nomination. Jackson was originally born in South Carolina to a single mother. He was elected student body president and played football while in college. It was during this time that he became active in local civil rights protests, particularly focusing on segregation in libraries, theatres, and restaurants. Because of these experiences, he became a part of the Greenville Eight when he was arrested while participating in a sit-in at the Greenville Public Library that was solely for the use of white people. He then began working with Dr. King and participated in the Selma marches as well as many other essential movements. He took part in many national and international political coalitions, eventually leading to his nomination for the presidency by the Democratic Party in 1984 and 1988. Jackson has become a political paragon, using his influence to turn the black vote out and for protesting unjust causes.

Then, in the 2008 elections, Barack Obama (1961) was the first African American ever elected President. Obama was born in Hawaii to an American and Kenyan family. He went on to attend Columbia University, after several years as a community activist. He moved to Chicago, spent three years there before enrolling at Harvard Law School in 1988. He stated that he saw the law as a vehicle to facilitate better community organization and activism. In 1990 in *Ebony Magazine,* he stated: "The idea was not only to get people to hope and dream, but to know how the tax structure affects what kind of housing gets built."

Based on his grades and writings, he was selected as assistant editor of the *Harvard Law Review*, the most prestigious law review in the nation. Two years later, he became the first ever black editor of the *Harvard Law* Review, which is considered the highest student position at Harvard Law School. He became known as one of the most brilliant law students during his time at Harvard.

It was also at Harvard, where he met his brilliant wife, Michelle (1964). He worked as a community organizer and then a civil rights attorney before launching his political career. He became a senator for Illinois, and later became the first African American President of the United States, and achieved great attention for his landslide victory and massive popularity.

His inauguration was a showcase of strong and powerful black culture, with performances by Aretha Franklin and Beyoncé and readings by Maya Angelou. President Barak Obama would prove to be an intelligent, compassionate leader of integrity, and a loving husband and endearing father. During his first term in office, he focused closely on the Affordable Care Act, making sure that this essential healthcare reform bill passed and was signed into law. He also passed the Dodd-Frank Wall Street Reform and Consumer Protection Act to tighten regulations on banks after the 2008 recession. He

built coalitions with allies abroad and worked to try to end the wars in Iraq and Afghanistan. He governed exceptionally, with no major political or sexual scandals during his eight years in office.

Outside of the political giants, thousands of black activists who have used their lives to bring justice and equality to African Americans. For example, Alicia Garza, Patrisse Cullors, and Opal Tometi all founded the Black Lives Matter (BLM) movement following the murders of unarmed black men, women, and children by police, mentioned earlier. Alicia Garza (1981) is a civil rights activist and a journalist who has focused on domestic laborers' rights, police brutality, and transgender rights. She lives in Oakland, where she continues to build momentum for the movement. Patrisse Cullors (1984) is a noted artist and activist who has used her work to fight for justice reform and queer rights. She brings attention to the different challenges faced by queer black individuals and their vulnerabilities. Opal Tometi is a Nigerian-American human and civil rights activist who focuses on immigration reform and racial justice. She commonly appears on media outlets and uses her writings to communicate and advocate.

Another recent seminal movement exposing violence was founded also by a black woman named Tarana Burke (1973). Burke responded to the pervasive use of sexual violence and secret abuse with the simple but powerful hashtag and phrase "me too," founding the #metoo movement. This movement focused media attention on the pervasive sexual violence in nearly every discipline and field. She developed the phrase in order to call attention to the fact that nearly every woman has faced some form of sexual violence or harassment. She was named the *Time* Person of the Year for 2017.

CHAPTER REVIEW

1. Stokey Carmichael participated in which movement?
    a. Civil Rights
    b. Pan-Africanism
    c. Black Power
    d. All of the above

2. Jesse Jackson is known for:
    a. His leadership of the Black Panthers
    b. Being the first African American man elected President
    c. Being the first African American man to receive the nomination for President
    d. Being the first African American man to receive the nomination for Vice President

3. Barack Obama is known for:
    a. His leadership of the Black Panthers
    b. Being the first African American man elected President
    c. Being the first African American man to receive the nomination for President
    d. Being the first African American man to receive the nomination for Vice President

4. Obama's significant policies from his first term include:
    a. The healthcare reform bill named the Affordable Care Act
    b. The Dodd-Frank Wall Street Reform and Consumer Protection Act
    c. Trying to end the wars in Iraq and Afghanistan.
    d. All of the above

5. Alicia Garza, Patrisse Cullors, and Opal Tometi founded:
    a. The Black Panther Party
    b. The #metoo Movement
    c. Black Lives Matter
    d. The SNCC

6. TRUE or FALSE: Stokey Carmichael turned down a full ride to Harvard to attend Howard University
    a. True
    b. False

CHAPTER 4

ART

The five decades from the 1970s to the 2010s have been times of exuberance and exploration for African American visual artists and musicians.

As a painter, writer, sculptor, and performance artist, Faith Ringgold (1930) quickly became an avid storyteller through her many different forms of expression. Born in Harlem, her parents had come to New York City by way of the Great Migration. She quickly became acquainted with some of the biggest names of the Harlem Renaissance and enrolled an art program. In spite of her incredibly diverse skill, she became most well-known for her quilt paintings, and her contributions continue to live on as an important form of storytelling.

From a more formal tradition, Simmie Knox (1935) became an important portrait artist during this period. Knox was born in Alabama and grew up on a sharecropper farm. He began drawing after he was hit in the eye by a baseball. The nuns who taught him at school recognized his talent and found him an art tutor, as art classes were not offered to the segregated school at that time. He went on to attend university, studying textiles and art, where he began painting still life pieces. His work was noticed by famous African Americans, such as Muhammed Ali and Thurgood Marshall. He painted well-known portraits of the many interesting figures making history during this time. He was then invited by the

White House to be the first African American to paint a President when he painted the portraits of Bill and Hillary Clinton. His work lives on in his portrayals of these notable figures.

Photography as art also changed and expanded its possibilities, as Lorna Simpson (1960) used mixed mediums with her photographs to convey meaningful messages. Simpson was born in Brooklyn, NY, where she was exposed from an early age to the vibrant art and theatre scene of New York City. She showed at the Museum of Modern Art (MOMA) in New York, and also developed forms of performance art through film. Her work defied societal constructions of race, culture, sexuality, and identity, as her piece *Neckline* demonstrates. The piece depicts two necks and then lists words affiliated with lynching with the final sentence at the bottom reading "*feel the ground sliding from under you.*"

In painting, Jean-Michel Basquiat (1960-1988) has become one of the most infamous artists of the twentieth century. Basquiat was born in Brooklyn to Haitian and Puerto Rican parents, he began making art from an extremely young age such as when he and a friend began spraying graffiti throughout New York City, and signing their images and phrases SAMO. He burst onto the art scene with his wild and imaginative paintings that depicted vulnerable bodies under the strain of dichotomy, such as wealth and poverty or integration and segregation. He used expressionist forms to communicate criticisms about the power structures of the United States and to interrogate the role of the individual. Tragically, Basquiat died from a heroin overdose, at the young age of 27. One of his paintings was sold for the highest price ever garnished at auction for painting, at over $100 million dollars.

Born nearly a decade after Basquiat, Kara Walker (1969) is a prolific painter, filmmaker, and installation artists. Born in California, she learned about art from her father, who was a painter. Her pieces usually involved commentaries about the social and sexual violence that occurred in the plantation south, and challenged stereotypes using her minimalist presentation. Her work is displayed at some of the best museums in the world.

As highly successful newcomers, Titus Kaphar (1976) and Kehinde Wiley (1977) both used different styles of portraiture to communicate important truths about the black experience in art history and at the turn of the century. Kaphar was born in Michigan, where he taught himself how to paint after attending an art history course during his undergraduate degree, where his professor skipped the section on African American art history. He used this concept as his jumping-off point, creating works that made black experiences throughout the history of art extremely visible and powerful. He went on to receive his MFA from Yale University. He challenged historical power dynamics and reproduced classical pieces to redirect the viewers' attention onto the injustices of the time. He also won the MacArthur Genius Grant in 2018.

Kehinde Wiley was born in California to an American mother but traveled to Nigeria at the age of twenty to meet his father and explore his roots. He returned to earn his MFA from Yale University, where he began to make his name using a combination of traditional portraiture and contemporary methods of representation. Moving to New York City, he used art history and the individuals he observed in Harlem as an inspiration for challenging classical styles of painting. For example, he used a portrait of Napoleon to comment on the dynamics of power and race. His status as a master artist was further boosted when he was commissioned to paint a portrait of President Barack Obama, which now hangs in the Smithsonian.

THE AGE OF RECKONING 1977 - 2019

CHAPTER REVIEW

1. Faith Ringgold is best known for creating:
    a. Storytelling quilts
    b. Portraits
    c. Shadow puppets
    d. Collage with text

2. Simmie Knox's family were sharecroppers, and although he was very talented, he was elevated to fame once he painted?
    a. Collages with text
    b. Being the first African American to paint a U.S. President (President Bill & Hilary Clinton). He was invited to the White House where is painted their portrait.
    c. Shadow puppets
    d. Beautiful city landscapes

3. Kara Walker used art to commentaries to express the social and sexual violence that occurred in the plantation south. What did she also use her art to challenge?
    a. Race relations
    b. Relationships
    c. Politics
    d. Stereotypes

4. Basquiat is known for using his painting to express?
    a. SAMO graffiti
    b. His painting being sold at auction for the highest rate of any painting
    c. The strain of dichotomy, such as wealth and poverty or integration and segregation
    d. All of the above

5. Titus Kaphar is known for:
    a. His challenging of art history
    b. Making black experiences visible
    c. Winning the Macarthur Genius Grant
    d. All of the above

6. Kehinde Wiley was a well know painter, but his status was boosted when he painted:
    a. Napoleon
    b. Barack Obama
    c. Bill Clinton
    d. All of the above

CHAPTER 5

LITERATURE

African Americans also made great and invaluable contributions to literature and writing from the 1970s to the 2010s. Journalism, television, popular fiction, and other fields benefited greatly from these voices.

As one of the first African Americans to draw attention to African American history on a popular scale, Alex Haley (1921-1992) wrote *Roots* as well as an autobiography about Malcolm X. He was born in New York and enlisted in the U.S. Coast Guard during World War II where he began crafting incredible stories for his fellow officers. After the war, he transitioned to journalism when he became the senior editor for *Reader's Digest*. He went on to interview famous jazz musician Miles Davis followed by his extensive research on the life trajectory of Malcolm X. This biography remains the seminal text on the important leader. He then published his novel, *Roots: The Saga of an American Family*, which was a story based on his own family's history of enslavement. He won the Pulitzer Prize for this novel, and it was eventually made into a television series on ABC depicting the traumas of slavery and the history of African Americans, as mentioned in greater detail in the opening to this chapter. Haley's work remains central today, and *Roots* was readapted into a second series in 2016.

In the field of journalism, Robert C. Maynard (1937-1993) became an essential editor and founder of many notable publications in the United States. Maynard was born in New York, where he was noticed early on for his writing capabilities. Maynard received a fellowship to study journalism at Harvard University, and then joined the editorial staff of *The Washington Post*. After making his career in journalism, he moved to California, where he took over as editor and later, owner, of the *Oakland Tribune*, becoming the first African American to own a major metropolitan newspaper. His work transformed the newspaper into a Pulitzer Prize-winner. He also co-founded an institute for journalism education, which has trained over 1000 journalists in the United States.

Bill Garth was the guiding force behind the largest African American owned ABC audited newspaper in America. Citizen Newspapers had a total combined circulation of 121,000 and a weekly readership of 400,000, primarily in the Chicago region, whose population was close to 50% African American at the time. He became the first African American to be elected President of the Illinois Press Association. As a philanthropist, in 1995 he established the Quentis Bernard Garth (Q.B.G.) Foundation, which provides scholarships to disenfranchised inner-city youths in the Chicago area, and has disbursed over $1 million in scholarships thus far.

Taking an activist approach, Yolande Cornelia "Nikki" Giovanni (1943) works as one of the most well-known poets in the United States, in addition to her role as a writer, commentator, and educator. Born in Tennessee, she went on to study literature at Fisk University before even finishing high school. Facing the loss of her grandmother, Giovanni began to write poetry to cope with her death. These poems later became the infamous work *Black Feelings, Black Talk*. This work was inspired by the Civil Rights and the Black Power movements and reached millions of readers through her incredible portrayals of black women. She went on to teach, continues to write, and appear on television from time to time, discussing issues important to African Americans.

Alice Walker (1944) also burst onto the literary scene, writing one of the most important contemporary African American novels. Born in Georgia, Walker became the valedictorian of her high school and went on to attend Sarah Lawrence College. She became known for her poetry, which she used to process her feelings about many different aspects of her life, such as occurred in her work *Once*. Her most acclaimed piece, *The Color Purple*, which tells the story of a young black woman surviving racism and patriarchy. It was adapted into a play, and then became a critically acclaimed film starring Oprah Winfrey and Whoopi Goldberg.

In a completely different genre, Octavia Butler (1947-2006) became a Master of Science fiction. Born in California, Butler struggled with dyslexia and felt extremely shy as a child. She found solace in reading, quickly becoming interesting in science fiction. She went on to study at UCLA and attended a workshop of science fiction writers, where she sold her first stories for publication in an anthology. Over the next five years, Butler dedicated her attention to a series of novels known as the Patternist series. She achieved acclaim when she wrote "Speech Sounds," which won the Hugo Award for short story. She went on to write many more exciting series, such as the *Fledgling* series, eventually becoming the first science fiction writer to win the MacArthur Fellowship.

Returning to the deeply personal, Maya Angelou (1928-2014) has been named one of the greatest African American authors. Born in Missouri, her first novel *I Know Why the Caged Bird Sings* recounted the struggle, victories, and abuse that she had lived through during her childhood. She worked in many different roles, including fry cook, sex worker, journalist, and actor. She also was an activist during the Civil Rights Movement and worked closely with both Martin Luther King Jr. as well as Malcolm X. Her novels have been deemed autobiographical fiction or pure autobiography. Her incredible talent fashioned her as a spokesperson for black women and allowed her to challenge racism and sexual violence. She has been nominated for numerous awards, such as the Pulitzer Prize, and her books continue to be read throughout the world.

Finally, the work of Toni Morrison (1931) has remained equally foundational and moving in her prolific writing career. Born in Ohio, Morrison grew up listening to folklore and to family histories, later attending Howard University and Cornell University. She began writing while at school, becoming a cornerstone of black intellectualism in her academic circles. Her second novel, *Sula,* was nominated for the National Book Award while her third, *Song of Solomon,* was received with national acclaim as well, winning her the National Book Critics Circle Award. Following these writings, Morrison began to publish her most celebrated work, *Beloved.* This novel tells the true story of an enslaved woman throughout her life in the South. This work was met with extreme success from fellow authors as well as from *The New York Times* and other critics. She won the Pulitzer Prize for fiction, as well as the Anisfield-Wolf Book Award. *Beloved* was transferred to a film that received acclaim, and which starred Oprah Winfrey. Morrison has gone on to teach at Princeton, where she has continued to write and teach. Overall, Morrison has illuminated some of the most painful and intimate aspects of black female existence.

AFRICAN AMERICAN HISTORY

CHAPTER REVIEW

1. Who was Alex Haley?
    a. He was the senior editor of Readers Digest
    b. He wrote *Roots*
    c. He wrote *The Autobiography of Malcolm X*
    d. All of the above

2. Richard C. Maynard was known early for his writing talent and went to:
    a. Received a fellowship to study journalism at Harvard
    b. Joined the editorial staff at the Washington Post
    c. He became the owner of the Oakland Tribune
    d. All of the above

3. "Nikki" Giovanni wrote:
    a. *The Color Purple*
    b. *Roots*
    c. *Black Feelings, Black Talk*
    d. The Fledgling Series

4. Alice Walker was Valedictorian of her class and went on to write which acclaimed novel?
    a. *The Color Purple*
    b. *Roots*
    c. *Black Feelings, Black Talk*
    d. The Fledgling Series

5. Octavia Butler wrote:
    a. *The Color Purple*
    b. *Roots*
    c. *Black Feelings, Black Talk*
    d. The Fledgling Series

6. Octavia Butler struggled with dyslexia but went on to study a UCLA and was:
    a. The first African American to win a Pulitzer Prize for literature
    b. The first African American to own a major metropolitan newspaper
    c. The first writer to win the MacArthur Fellowship for science fiction
    d. None of the above

7. Maya Angelou wrote:
    a. *I Know Why the Caged Bird Sings*
    b. *Beloved*
    c. *The Color Purple*
    d. *Song of Solomon*

8. Toni Morris attended Howard and Cornell Universities.
    a. *She won the* National Book Award
    b. *She won the National Book Critics Award*
    c. *She won the* Pulitzer Prize for fiction
    d. All of the above

CHAPTER 6

SPORTS

Bill Russell (1934) overcame the racism that he faced while competing to become one of the most successful basketball players of all time. In high school, his classmates threw rocks and trash at him while he played baseball for the school. Undeterred, he played for the Boston Celtics and became the powerhouse on the team, winning eleven NBA championships. His strengths were in his rebounds and his man-to-man defenses. He was the first player to achieve superstar status in the NBA. For his achievements, President Obama presented him with the Presidential Medal of Freedom in 2011 for his work on the court and in the Civil Rights Movement, clearing the way for the many extremely talented players who would come after him.

Following in his footsteps, Michael Jordan (1963) a true leader in every sense of the word was named the greatest North American athlete of the 20th Century by ESPN for his accomplishments which include six NBA Finals Most Valuable Player (MVP) Awards, ten scoring titles (both all-time records), five MVP Awards, ten All-NBA First Team designations, nine All-Defensive First Team honors, fourteen NBA All-Star Game selections, three All-Star Game MVP Awards, three steals titles, and the 1988 NBA Defensive Player of the Year Award. He holds the NBA records for highest career regular season scoring average (30.12 points per game) and highest career playoff scoring average (33.45 points per game). Along with his partnership with Nike, Brand Jordan, which has had over $1 billion in sales, branding him an astute businessman and the most marketed sport figure in history. He donates millions and millions of dollars to organizations like the Friends of the Children; the Hurricane Florence Response Fund; The Make A Wish Foundation; the Smithsonian's National Museum of African American History and Culture in Washington, DC; NAACP Legal Defense Fund and the International Association of Chiefs of Police just to name a few. His commitment to helping others and supporting the community has exemplifies the character traits of a true champion and leader.

Wilma Rudolph (1940-1994) was a world-renowned sprinter. Born in Tennessee, she became a world-record-holding Olympic champion. She competed in the 200-meter dash and won Gold medals during the Olympic Games in Australia and Italy. Her success made her a role model and a highly visible example of black female excellence. She gave voice to civil rights concerns and dedicated herself to educating and coaching other young black athletes.

Other outstanding African American athletes have continued to take on the cause of black liberation, power, and equality. This is the case with Colin Kaepernick (1987), whose peaceful "take a knee" protest set off a wave of national controversy. Kaepernick was born in Wisconsin before moving to California. He excelled at nearly every sport that he played and achieved a 4.0 GPA. He became an instant success while playing football in college at the University of Nevada. He became a quarterback for the San Francisco 49ers' after the team's starting quarterback was injured. In 2016, Kaepernick began to sit during the U.S. national anthem, commonly played before football games. He did so to call attention to racial injustice and police brutality. He began to symbolically kneel during the anthem in protest of this violence and to call attention to the many unarmed African American men, women, and children who were not protected from this racism. His actions shocked the football world and even extended to the political world, where President Trump attacked Kaepernick via Twitter for his peaceful protest for a better

America. For his protest, Kaepernick was effectively shut out of the NFL before he reached a settlement. Yet he stood up for what he felt was right, and ultimately prevailed against the NFL, by getting the NFL to agree to a multimillion-dollar settlement. Although he was able to bring these injustice front and center and to the attention of the entire nation, many argued that he should have used other methods to make this point.

LeBron James is another notable NBA player who is well known not only as a result of this accomplishment on the court which include, three NBA championships, four NBA Most Valuable Player Awards, three NBA Finals MVP Awards, and two Olympic gold medals but also for his community service. He is an active supporter of non-profit organizations, including After-School All-Stars, Boys & Girls Clubs of America, and Children's Defense Fund. His own charity foundation, the LeBron James Family Foundation, has partnered with the University of Akron to provide scholarships for as many as 2,300 children beginning in 2021. In 2016, he donated $2.5 million to the Smithsonian National Museum of African American History and Culture to support an exhibit on Muhammad Ali. In 2017, he received the J. Walter Kennedy Citizenship Award from the NBA for his "outstanding service and dedication to the community. In November of that same year, the Akron School Board approved the "I Promise School", a public elementary school created in a partnership with the LeBron James Family Foundation to help struggling elementary school students stay in school.

Two of the best women tennis players in the world today are sisters, Venus Williams and Serena Williams. Both of the Williams sisters have been ranked Number 1 in the world at some point in their tennis career. Between 2000 and 2016, they collectively won 12 Wimbledon singles titles (Venus won five, and Serena won seven). Their achievement was summed up by tennis.com in this way: "No other tennis players in the Open era have represented this country so brilliantly, for so long, with so little company at the top."

Finally, Tiger Woods was the first golfer in history to simultaneously hold all four PGA titles, and the youngest to win the Augusta National. In 2019, he added a fifth win of the Masters to his lifetime of achievement, in a performance that Michael Jordan has called "the greatest comeback I have ever seen." There are far too many amazing and astounding athletes to list in these few pages, but one obvious standout is clear, great achievements can be realized in any area thinkable with hard work, dedication, and determination.

CHAPTER REVIEW

1. Bill Russell was known for:
    a. His exceptional skills in basketball
    b. Winning the Presidential Medal of Freedom
    c. His participation in the Civil Rights Movement
    d. All of the above

2. Michael Jordan is well known for?
    a. Being a leader in the community
    b. Being an astute businessman
    c. Being one of the best basketball players of all time
    d. All of the Above

3. Wilma Rudolph won Olympic Gold Medals in Australia and Italy in which field?
    a. Football player
    b. Basketball player
    c. Track and field runner
    d. Baseball player

4. This athlete decided to take a stand for a better America but was horribly misunderstood?
    a. Colin Kaepernick
    b. LeBron James
    c. Wilma Rudolph
    d. Bill Russell

5. Who made history by holding all four PGA titles, and was the youngest to win the Augusta National
    a. Rory McIlroy
    b. Phil Mickelson
    c. Jordan Spieth
    d. Tiger Woods

CHAPTER 7

MATH AND SCIENCE

African Americans continued their successes in math and sciences careers between the 1970s and 2010s. They became inventors, scientists, mathematicians, and astronauts, making some of the most impressive scientific advancements in the world.

James Edward Maceo West (1931) became an important inventor, holding over 250 foreign and U.S. patents. West was born in Virginia, and quickly cultivated an interest in science. He graduated from Temple University with a degree in Physics, and then went on to work at Johns Hopkins University. His main inventions are in the foil electret microphone, in improving hearing aid technology, and in improvements in telephones, cameras, hearing aids, and baby monitors. He also has become a great advocate for diversity in science and technology, founding the Association of Black Laboratory Employees.

Similarly, Lonnie Johnson (1949) is also an inventor and engineer who holds over 120 patents. Born in Alabama, he was interested in science as a child and went on to join the U.S. Air Force, which led to his joining NASA. He is a trained nuclear engineer. He has worked collaboratively across universities on making electricity more environmentally friendly and affordable. One of his most profitable and well-known inventions was the Super Soaker water gun, which is one of the bestselling toys each year.

As another example of African American excellence, Guion Bluford (1942) became the first African American to go into space as a NASA astronaut. He was born in Pennsylvania and earned his Bachelors and Master's degree in Aerospace Engineering from Pennsylvania State University. He then became an Air Force pilot, where he continued to study flight dynamics. By 1979, he was chosen as an astronaut for NASA, out of thousands of potential candidates. He was a member of the team on four Space Shuttle flights, as a member of the crew of the Orbiter *Challenger* mission.

Bluford was followed into space by Mae Carol Jemison, the first African American woman to travel into space. Jemison (1956) was born in Alabama and felt attracted to the sciences, seeing Dr. King's speeches as a call to action for black excellence and bravery. She became a student at Stanford University at the age of sixteen.

After obtaining her M.D. at Cornell, she took a placement with the Peace Corps in Liberia and Sierra Leone as a medical officer. Inspired by Lieutenant Uhura on "Star Trek," she successfully applied to become an astronaut. She assisted with launch support at the Kennedy Space Center and then, in 1992, she flew her only space mission. She conducted experiments about the effect of weightlessness on the body. She continues to teach at Cornell and Dartmouth and also conducts research. She has founded space camps for children and has helped to make science education more accessible.

Dr. Philip Emeagwali, originally from Nigeria, has been called the Bill Gates of Africa, and a "Father of the Internet." In 1985, he used 65,000 processors to create the world's fastest computer. He won the Gorden Bell Prize – the Nobel Prize for computation. His computers are currently being used to forecast the weather and impacts of global warming.

Gladys West (b. 1930) leveraged her mathematical and programming expertise to invent an accurate model of the Earth, which was used as the foundation for the creation of the Global Positioning System (GPS).

Finally, Neil deGrasse Tyson (1958) is perhaps one of the most well-known astrophysicists and science educators. Born in New York City, Tyson began studying science from a young age and had a passion for the stars. He obsessively studied astronomy as he grew up, and received a hand-written letter of acceptance to Cornell University by famous astrophysicist Carl Sagan. Instead, he attended Harvard, where he began to collaborate with NASA and other astronomy organizations. He became the Director of the Hayden Planetarium, where he first fell in love with astrophysics, and also actively takes part in research and science education. He has written many books about science for the public, and also runs a science education podcast, named Star Talk Radio. He has starred in science education series on PBS and has worked with National Geographic. Tyson was awarded the Public Welfare Medal in 2015 by the U.S. National Academy of Sciences for his incredible ability to both make contributions to the field while also capturing the public imagination and interest about science.

The North Star is your guide point, said the conductors on the Underground Railroad, centuries ago. In the 500-plus years since the first free African American set foot on our shores, and the first African slaves were forcibly dragged to our shores, African Americans have shared the common threads of racism and inequality, but also the common threads of resilience, heroism, and achievement. We hold in our hands, and contribute to, the never-ending patchwork quilt of African American history - in this land we call the United States of America, and in its mix of unfinished promises, broken dreams, and ever-hopeful aspirations. We are each piece of its fabric: getting an education, deciding on a career, raising a family,

and making all the choices we make to create a good life. When our destiny or path seems unclear, we can reflect on the threads of our past and the accomplishments of our ancestors and remember we are the continuation of the threads they had woven, and search the sky for the North Star for strength and guidance.

Benjamin Solomon Carson Sr., born in 1951 in Detroit Michigan, is an American politician, author and former neurosurgeon serving as the 17th and current United States Secretary of Housing and Urban Development since 2017. He was a candidate for

<u>President of the United States</u> in the <u>Republican primaries in 2016</u>. He gained fame for his groundbreaking work, separating conjoined twins and being the director of pediatric neurosurgery at John Hopkins Hospital at the age of 33. Dr. Carson grew up in a poor household where his mother dropped out of school in the third grade and often worked two to three jobs concurrently in order to make ends meet. Although Dr. Carson had limited resources, in an environment which cultivated academic achievement, Carson excelled and was able to realize his dream of becoming a doctor. His excellent eye-hand coordination and three-dimensional reasoning skills made him a superior surgeon, and before long, he would become the chief resident in neurosurgery at John Hopkins. John Hopkins holds the spot for the #1 and #2 nursing and medical schools in the country respectively, and among the top three in hospitals for adult care.

CHAPTER REVIEW

1. James West had over 20 patents and know for improving hearing aid technology, and in improvements in telephones, cameras, hearing aids, and baby monitors. He inventions were?
    a. The super soaker
    b. Inventions related to audio technology
    c. An astronomy podcast
    d. All of the above

2. Lonnie Johnson was a nuclear engineer and invented?
    a. The super soaker
    b. Inventions related to audio technology
    c. An astronomy podcast
    d. All of the above

3. Guion Bluford is known for:
    a. Being the first African American woman in space
    b. Being the first African American man to go into space
    c. Being the head of the Hayden Planetarium
    d. Being the host of *Star Talk Radio*

4. Mae Carol Jemison is known for:
    a. Being the first African American woman in space
    b. Being the first African American man to go into space
    c. Being the head of the Hayden Planetarium
    d. Being the host of *Star Talk Radio*

5. Neil deGrasse Tyson is known for:
    a. Being the first African American woman in space
    b. Being the first African American man to go into space
    c. Inventing the Super Soaker
    d. Being the host of *Star Talk Radio*

6. Neil deGrasse Tyson is a (n):
    a. Biologist
    b. Engineer
    c. Inventor
    d. Astrophysicist

7. Who focused on science education?
    a. Guion Bluford
    b. Neil deGrasse Tyson
    c. Mae Jemison
    d. All of the above

8. Dr. Ben Carson is known for being a brilliant surgeon with stellar eye/ hand coordination?
    a. True
    b. False

AFRICAN AMERICAN HISTORY

ADDITIONAL REFERENCES ... AND FOR A "DEEPER DIVE"

The Autobiography of Malcolm X: As Told to Alex Haley

By Malcolm X

There Is a River: The Black Struggle for Freedom in America

By Vincent Harding

Our Kind of People

By Malcolm X

Between the World and Me

By Ta-Nehisi Coates

Why Should White Guys Have All the Fun?: How Reginald Lewis Created a Billion-Dollar Business Empire

By Reginald F. Lewis, Blair S. Walker

Boss: The Black Experience in Business

Stanley Nelson (Director) Rated: PG Format: DVD

Black America Since MLK: And Still I Rise

Rated: PG Format: DVD

The Mis-Education of the Negro

By Carter Godwin Woodson

Hollywood Black (Turner Classic Movies): The Stars, the Films, the Filmmakers

By Donald Bogle (Author), John Singleton (Foreword)

The Wealth Choice: Success Secrets of Black Millionaires Kindle Edition

By Dennis Kimbro

JAY-Z: Made in America

By Michael Eric Dyson

The Power of Broke: How Empty Pockets, a Tight Budget, and a Hunger…

By Daymond John

APPENDIX 1

SOURCES

DISCLAIMER ON IMAGES – We have made a good faith effort to research and cite all images used in this text. Based on our research, it is our belief that all of the images used in this text are copyright free, with free permission to republish. If we are made aware of any copyrighted images inadvertently used in this text, we will pull both the image and its citation here upon written receipt and claim of active copyright.

Time Period 1: The "Pre-United States" Days, 1513-1774

Juan Garrido Speaks

Details used in this first-person narrative were culled from the following sources:

Henry Louis Gates, Jr. "Who Was the First African American?" The Root, 10/22/12. Online link: https://www.theroot.com/who-was-the-first-african-american-1790893808

Author unspecified. "Juan Garrido, Hernán Cortés, and Mexico City." augustine.com. Online link: https://www.visitstaugustine.com/history/black_history/juan_garrido/mexico_city.php

Erica L. Taylor, The Tom Joyner Morning Show, 11/5/2013. "Little Known Black History Fact: Juan Garrido." Online link: https://blackamericaweb.com/2013/11/05/little-known-black-history-fact-juan-garrido/

Time Period 1 Text

Research used in the creation of Time Period 1 text was from a variety of public sources, including the following:

Slavery Timeline, 1501-1600, A Chronology of Slavery, Abolition, and Empancipation in the Sixteenth Century. Online link: www.brycchancarey.com

Joe Carter. "5 Facts about the transatlantic slave trade," in ERLC, Aug 17, 2018. Online link: https://erlc.com/resource-library/articles/5-facts-about-the-transatlantic-slave-trade

Michael Guasco, "The Misguided Focus on 1619 as the Beginning of Slavery in the U.S. Damages Our Understanding of American History." smithsonian.com, September 13, 2017. Online link: https://www.smithsonianmag.com/history/misguided-focus-1619-beginning-slavery-us-damages-our-understanding-american-history-180964873/

Douglas T. Peck. "The Little Known Explorations of Lucas Vasquez de Ayllon That Set the Stage for European Conquest of North America." Research paper, no publication data. From the history archives of historian David Messineo.

The point that the number of African slaves who entered the United States was 380,000, or 4-6% of the total Trans-Atlantic Slave trade, came from this source:
Daina Ramey Berry, Associate Professor of History and African and African Diaspora Studies, University of Texas at Austin. "Slavery in America: back in the headlines." THE CONVERSATION (Academic rigor, journalistic flair), October 21, 2014. Online link: https://theconversation.com/slavery-in-america-back-in-the-headlines-33004

Time Period 1 Image Sources

Opening Image – Juan Garrido. 16th century painting. Image in the public domain.
Following the opening image, 9 additional images are used in Time Period 1.
Here are their citations:
1. Map, Africa.
2. Engraving, Jorge Biassou.
3. Map, St. Augustine.
4. Engraving, Slaves in Ship Cargo Hold.
5. Engraving by Scipio Morehead, "Phillis Wheatley."
6. Painting by Joshua Johnson, "The Westwood Children." The National Gallery of Art. Retrieved 2004-05-15.
7. Book Cover, *Olaudah Equiano*.
8. Engraving, Benjamin Banneker.

Chapter 2: A New Country, 1775-1800

Crispus Attucks Speaks

Details used in this first-person narrative were culled from the following sources:

"Crispus Attucks." PBS Thirteen, Africans in America Resource Bank. Online link: http://www.pbs.org/wgbh/aia/part2/2p24.html

"The History of Crispus Attucks as a Man." crispusattucks.org. Online link: http://crispusattucks.org/about/who-was-crispus-attucks/

Time Period 2 Text

Research used in the creation of Time Period 2 text was from a variety of public sources, including the following:

The 1794 research outlining space measurements for slave on slave ships is from:
Joe Carter. "5 Facts about the transatlantic slave trade," in ERLC, Aug 17, 2018. Online link: https://erlc.com/resource-library/articles/5-facts-about-the-transatlantic-slave-trade

Time Period 2 Image Sources

Opening Image – The Repeal or the Funeral Procession of Miss Americ-Stamp. Image in the public domain.

Following the opening image, 14 additional images are used in Time Period 2.

Here are their citations:
1. The Runaway. July 1837. Corpus Cripus. A common image used in runaway slave ads. From *The Underground Railroad from Slavery to Freedom* by Wilbur Henry Siebert, Albert Bushnell. Published by Macmillan, 1898, p 26.
2. The Boston Massacre.
3. Painting, circa 1793, Lafayette at Yorktown. Image of Marquis de Lafayette and James Armistead Lafayette. Lafayette College Art Collection. Image due to age believed to be in public domain.
4. Peter Salem.
5. Rev. Richard Allen.
6. Lemuel Haynes. Wikimedia Commons.
7. James Forten.
8. Black Regiment, Civil War.
9. African-American Quilt.
10. Slaves in Neck Chains and Shackles.
11. Slaves on Plantation, South Carolina.
12. Benjamin Banneker Almanac Cover, 1795.
13. Photo, Cotton Gin.
14. Thomas L. Jennings.

Time Period 3: Antebellum and the Civil War, 1801-1865

Harriet Tubman Speaks

Details used in this first-person narrative were culled from memory, from placards read and seen in 2018 at the National Park Service Harriet Tubman Underground Railroad Visitors Center. Author's note: Details such as Harriet Tubman singing to the slaves to calm them down, and slaves coming onto the gunboats with chickens in cages, are not fictional inventions, but actual historical events cited on the Visitor Center displays. Online link to the Center at:

https://news.maryland.gov/dnr/2017/02/28/harriet-tubman-underground-railroad-visitor-center/

Time Period 3 Text

Research used in the creation of Time Period 3 text was from a variety of public sources.

Adapted from Kenneth Marvin Hamilton, *Black Towns and Profit: Promotion and Development in the Trans-Appalachian West, 1877–1915* (Urbana, Ill., 1991); and Ben Wayne Wiley, Ebonyville in the South and Southwest: Political Life in the All-Black Town, Ph.D. diss., University of Texas at Arlington (1984).

Freedom's Journal, March 16, 1827. John B. Russwurm and Samuel Cornish, founders. Copyprint from microfilm. Microform Reading Room, General Collections, Library of Congress (2–9)

Hinks, Peter P. *To Awaken My Afflicted Brethren: David Walker and the Problem of Antebellum Slave Resistance*. Pennsylvania State University Press, 1996. ISBN 978-0271015798

Walker, David. *David Walker's Appeal*. Black Classics Press, 1997. ISBN 978-0933121386

Time Period 3 Image Sources

Opening Image – 1861/1863 Emancipation Proclamation. Image in the public domain. Following the opening image, 15 additional images are used in Time Period 3. Here are their citations:

1. Engraving, The Fight at Corney's Bridge, Bayou Teche, Louisiana, and Destruction of the Rebel Gun-boat "Cotton," January 14, 1863. Published in *Harper's Weekly*, 1863. U.S. Naval Historical Center Photograph. Photo #: NH 58767.
2. Harriet Tubman.
3. Photo, Slaves on Plantation, Aerial View. J.J. Smith's Plantation, South Carolina. 1862. Photographed by Timothy H. O'Sullivan. Getty Collection, via Google Cultural Institute.
4. Photo, Slaves in Field w/Wagon.
5. Statue, "El Yanga."
6. Photo, Miners During the Gold Rush, circa 1900. U.S. National Archives and Records Administration.
7. Painting, Denmark Vesey.
8. Painting, La Amistad.
9. Engraving, Resurrection of Husky Box Brown.
10. Photo, Underground Railroad.
11. 1835 Engraving, Chained Female Slave, by Patrick H. Reason. In the public domain.
12. 1864 Painting, "Meeting by the River" by Robert Seldon Duncanson. Williams College Museum of Art.
13. Frederick Douglass. Library of Congress.
14. 1852 Cover, *Uncle Tom's Cabin* by Harriet Beecher Stowe.
15. Engraving of Charles H. Reason.

Time Period 4: Reconstruction, 1866-1900

Abraham Lincoln Speaks

Details used in this first-person narrative were based on various sources and knowledge about Abraham Lincoln, culled over a lifetime of learning. Sections in quotations are the actual unembellished words of Abraham Lincoln, in speeches and narrative culled from:

Philip B. Kunhardt, Jr., Philip B. Kunhardt III, and Peter W. Kunhardt. *Lincoln: An Illustrated Biography*. New York, NY: Alfred A Knopf, 1992.

Legends and Lies, Season 1, Episode 9: "Bass Reeves: The Real Lone Ranger". Internet Movie Database. Retrieved 18 October 2015. *(https://encyclopediaofarkansas.net/entries/bass-reeves-1747/#)*

"Statue of U.S. marshal to travel from Oklahoma to Arkansas Wednesday", Associated Press in *The Oklahoman*, 16 May 2012 (pay site).)

Time Period 4 Text

Research used in the creation of Time Period 4 text was from a variety of public sources.

Time Period 4 Image Sources

Opening Image – Photo of Lincoln Statue, "To Bind The Nation's Wounds." Image in public domain. Following the opening image, 22 additional images are used in Time Period 4.
Here are their citations:

1. Colored Men. The First Americans Who Planted Our Flag.
2. Some of our Brave Colored Boys Who Helped Free Cuba.
3. Discovery of Nat Turner.
4. The First Colored Senator and Representatives.
5. Photo, African-American Cowboys.
6. Photo, Mary Fields, circa 1895. In the public domain. Source: http://www.reunionblackfamily.com/apps/blog/show/14748608-mary-fields-started-life-as-a-slave-in-freedom-after-the-civil-war
7. Photo, Bass Reeves.
8. Photo, Tuskeegee Institute Gateway. Wikepedia. Creative Commons attribution.
9. Photo, Benjamin Davis Oliver
10. Photo, Frederick Douglass
11. Photo, W.E.B. DuBois.
12. Photo, Mary McLeod Bethune.
13. Photo by Cornelius Marion Battey. Wikepedia.
14. Photo, W.C. Handy.
15. Photo, Scott Joplin. Library of Congress.
16. Photo, Harriet Ann Jacobs.
17. Photo, William Stanley Beaumont Braithwaite.
18. Photo, George Washington Carver.
19. Photo, Ernest Everett Just.
20. Photo, Andrew J. Beard.
21. Photo, Lewis Howard Lattimer.
22. Book Cover, *The Life of Daniel Hale Williams*.

Time Period 5: The Road to Greater Equality, 1901-1976

Rosa Parks Speaks

Details used in this first-person narrative were culled from the following sources:

"Rosa Parks." Article on The History Channel website. Online link: https://www.history.com/topics/black-history/rosa-parks

Time Period 5 Text

Research used in the creation of Time Period 4 text was from a variety of public sources, along with the following:

Recollections of Martha Reeves are from:
Martha Reeves and Mark Bego. *Dancing in the Street: Confessions of a Motown Diva* (1974).

Time Period 5 Image Sources

Opening Image – Photo, Martin Luther King at March on Washington, 1964. Army Reserve Photo Gallery.
Following the opening image, 30 additional images are used in Time Period 5.
Here are their citations:

1. Photo, Rosa Parks. U.S. National Archives and Records Administration.
2. Photo, Carter Godwin Woodson.
3. Photo, Wide Lens. Black Wall Street. Greenwood Community, Tulsa, Oklahoma. Creative Commons.
4. 4-photo square. Greenwood, Tulsa, Oklahoma. Black Tulsa City by Clarence Jack.
5. Photo, Community on Fire.
6. Photo, Negro Residence After Fire.
7. Engraving, The Hamburg Riot, July 1876.
8. Photo, Protest Against Race Mixing.
9. Photo, Children, Integrated.
10. Photo, Freedom Riders.
11. Photo, Lunch Counter Sit-In.
12. Photo, March Signs.
13. Photo, Triple Nickel. "Members of the 555th (Triple Nickel) Parachute Infantry Battalion are briefed before take-off from Fort Dix in New Jersey in 1947." Image is work of a U.S. Department of Agriculture employee, taken or made as part of that person's official duties. As a work of the U.S. Federal Government, the image is in the public domain. Source: 20111110-OC-AMW-0004.
14. Photo, Ida B. Wells.
15. Photo, Josephine Baker. Photographed by Carl VanVechten, October 20, 1949. From the collection of the Library of Congress and in the public domain: http://memory.loc.gov/ammen/vvhtml/vvres.html
16. Photo, Martin Luther King at March on Washington, 1964. Army Reserve Photo Gallery.
17. Photo, Malcolm X.

18. Photo, Aaron Douglas.
19. Photo, Langston Hughes. Library of Congress, Prints & Photographs Division, Jack Delano. Under the digital id cph.3a43849.
20. Photo, James Baldwin. Wikipedia, under James Baldwin_37_Allan_Warren(cropped).jpg
21. Photo, John H. Robinson.
22. Photo, Billie Holiday, by William P. Gottlieb. Library of Congress, Music Division, digital id gottlieb.04211.
23. Photo, The Supremes. No known copyright.
24. Photo, George Poage in 1903.
25. Photo, Muhammed Ali. Photographer unknown. Dutch National Archives, The Hague, Fotocollectie Algemeen Nederlands Persbureau (ANEFO), 1945-1989.
26. Photo, Myrtis Dightman.
27. Photo, Percy Lavon Julian.
28. Photo, Garrett Augustus Morgan, Sr. Armed With Science website.
29. Photo, Henrietta Lacks.
30. Photo, Dr. Vivien T. Thomas. de.wikipedia.org.

Time Period 6: The Age of Reckoning, 1977-2019

A TV Executive Speaks

Details used in this first-person narrative were culled from memory of the author from first-person viewing of the ABC TV miniseries "Roots," and the social discussion that followed, in January 1977. Quotations on the ratings of "Roots" were culled from the Wikipedia page on "Roots." Kunta Kinte is a character from the novel by Alex Haley, *Roots: The Saga of an American Family*. New York, NY: Dell Publishing Co., Inc., 1976.

Time Period 6 Text

Research used in the creation of Time Period 6 text was from a variety of public sources.

Time Period 6 Image Sources

Opening Image – Photo, Barack Obama. This file is a work of an employee of the Executive Office of the President of the United States, taken or made as part of that person's official duties. As a work of the U.S. Federal Government, it is in the public domain.

Following the opening image, 27 additional images are used in Time Period 6. Here are their citations:
1. Photo, Nancy Reagan, "Just Say No." White House Photographic Office (1981-1989). U.S. National Archives and Record Administration.
2. Photo, African-American First Responders, September 11, 2001.
3. Photo, Oprah Winfrey, by Greg Hernandez from California, USA.
4. Photo, John Lewis.
5. Photo, Huey Newton. U.S. Department of Justice, Federal Bureau of Investigation. Record Group 65: Records of the Federal Bureau of Investigation, 1896-2008, Public Domain, https://commons.wikimedia.org/w/index.php?curid-66559222.

6. Photo, Angela Davis, by Bundesarchiv, Bild 183-L0911-029 / Koard, Peter / CC-BY-SA 3.0 de. Public Domain, https://commons.wikimedia.org/w/index.php?curid=55271874.
7. Photo, African-American Child with Caucasian Police Officer.
8. Photo, Police Officers.
9. Photo, Stokey Carmichael.
10. Photo, Jesse Jackson.
11. Photo, Barack and Michelle Obama. This file is a work of an employee of the Executive Office of the President of the United States, taken or made as part of that person's official duties. As a work of the U.S. Federal Government, it is in the public domain. Source: White House (021913PS-0395).
12. Photo, The Obama Family.
13. Photo, Jean-Michel Basquiat.
14. Painting, Kara Walker. Creative Commons in another language.
15. Photo, Image of the Kunta Kinte Alex Haley Memorial in Annapolis, MD, by Preservation Maryland, January 16, 2013. Creative Commons Attribution-Share-Alike 2.0 Generic License.
16. Photo, Robert C. Maynard. The copyright holder of this work has released it into the public domain.
17. Photo, Yolande Cornelia/Nikki Giovanni. CC By 2.5, https://en.wikipedia.org/w/index.php? curid=7667498
18. Photo, Bill Russell.
19. Photo, Michael Jordan.
20. Photo, Wilma Rudolph. National Archief. Wikimedia Commons.
21. Photo, Colin Kaepernick. "San Francisco 49ers vs. Green Bay Packers at Lambeau Field on September 9, 2012." Photo by Mike Morbeck. Uploaded to Commons by Moe Epsilon on December 15, 2013.
22. Photo, "LeBron James of the Cleveland Cavaliers in a game against the Washington Wizards at Verizon Center on November 21, 2014 in Washington, DC." Wikimedia Commons.
23. Photo, Venus and Serena Williams.
24. Photo, James Edward Maceo West. Creative Commons Attribution Share-Alike 4.0 International License.
25. Photo, Lonnie Johnson. Creative Commons Attribution 2.0 Generic License. Source: 160202-N-PO203-057.
26. Photo, Guion Bluford. Wikimedia Commons. Source: http://www.jsc.nasa.gov/Bios/htmlbios/bluford-gs.html
27. Photo, "Neil de Grasse Tyson signing a copy of his book *Origins*." Taken at JREF's TAM6, The Amazing Meeting. Copyright holder has released this work into the public domain.

APPENDIX 2

THE 35 BEST IN MOVIES AND TELEVISION,
FOR INTERESTING PORTRAYALS OF AFRICAN AMERICANS IN HISTORY

While there are many fictional movies featuring African-American characters, some change the actual history to suit the whims of the writer, director, producer, etc. The following movies are excellent on several levels: plot, characterization, cinematography, and especially their efforts to hone closely to the actual history, honoring the real stories of those who made a positive difference in the lives of many. This is not a complete list, but 30 of the best in movies and television, for accurate portrayals of African-American history, provided in alphabetical order (with some exception to historical accuracy noted in the text accompanying the listing):

A Raisin in the Sun (2008) - Based on the Pulitzer Prize-winning play by Lorraine Hansberry.

Ali (2001) - Biopic on Muhammed Ali, featuring Will Smith.

All the Way (2016) - HBO TV movie about the passage of the 1964 Civil Rights Act.

Amistad (1997) - True story of 1839 slave ship Amistad and its court case. Directed by Steven Spielberg.

Autobiography of Miss Jane Pittman (1974) - TV movie/fictionalized biography, with a wonderful star turn by Cicely Tyson in the leading role.

Birth of a Nation (2016) - Controversial story of the Nat Turner slave rebellion. Some debate as to historical accuracy, but great tackling of racism and white supremacy.

BlackKKlansman (2018) - Based on a true story. Directed by Spike Lee.

The Color Purple (1985) - Gut-wrenching film based on the 1983 Pulitzer Prize-winning novel by Alice Walker.

Dreamgirls (2006) - Fictional movie, loosely based on the story of The Supremes.

Fences (2016) - Fictional, based on August Wilson's 10-play Pittsburgh Cycle of African American history.

42 (2013) - Biopic on Jackie Robinson

Glory (1989) - Civil War movie about one of the first all-African-American regiments in the Union Army.

Green Book (2018) - Fictionalized story of an African-American classical pianist, touring through the South with a white driver. Period details are accurate, but substantial debate about the one-sided portrayal, primarily from the white driver's perspective.

Guess Who's Coming to Dinner (1967) - Fictional interracial comedy.

Harriet Tubman (2019). Lots of respected historians involved. High expectations.

The Help (2011) - Fictional story of an African American maid's work for a white family in the 1960s.

Hidden Figures (2016) - Biopic on African-American women contributing to NASA in the 1950s and 1960s

John Adams (2008) - TV Miniseries about John Adams, considered by some historians to be the most accurate depiction of events of the American Revolution ever filmed.

Lady Sings the Blues (1972) - Biopic about singer Billie Holliday, featuring Diana Ross.

Lee Daniels' The Butler (2013) - Biopic based on true story of White House Butler Cecil Gaines.

Love and Diane (2002) - Documentary about the Hazzard family of Brooklyn, NY, and the best documentary on an African-American family that you've likely never seen.

Loving (2016) - True story of the interracial couple who won a 1967 U.S. Supreme Court case.

Malcolm X (1992) - Fictionalized account of Malcolm X by director Spike Lee, featuring critically acclaimed performance by Denzel Washington.

Marshall (2017) - Biopic about U.S. Supreme Court Justice Thurgood Marshall.

Nine From Little Rock (1964) - Documentary about the Little Rock 9 and integration.

Precious (2009) - Fictional story of an African-American woman struggling with poverty and abuse.

Ray (2004) - Biopic on Ray Charles, featuring Jamie Foxx.

Remember the Titans (2000) - Biopic set in 1971, based on a true story.

Rosa Parks Story (2002) - TV movie about Rosa Parks, "Mother of the Civil Rights Movement."

Roots (TV Miniseries, 1977) - Nominated for 37 Primetime Emmy Awards, winner of 9 of them. "Must see TV."

Rosewood (1997) - Based on true story of the 1923 Rosewood massacre in Florida.

Selma (2014) - Based on true story of the 1965 Selma to Montgomery voting rights march.

Sounder (1972) - Fictional movie, set in the 1930s, about a black sharecropper family trying to survive in the Great Depression.

To Kill a Mockingbird (1962) - Fictional movie, based on Harper Lee's Pulitzer Prize-winning play.

12 Years A Slave (2013) - Adaptation of the 1853 slave narrative by Solomon Northrup, *Twelve Years a Slave*.

PRINT VERSION

Time Period 1 (1513-1774)

Chapter 1
1. d
2. d
3. c
4. c
5. a
6. a
7. d
8. c
9. d
10. d
11. c

Chapter 2
1. d
2. c
3. b
4. b
5. c
6. a
7. c

Chapter 3
1. b
2. a
3. a
4. b

Chapter 4
1. d
2. c
3. b
4. a
5. a
6. a
7. a
8. a
9. b

Chapter 5
1. c
2. a
3. d
4. c
5. c
6. b
7. c
8. d

Chapter 6
1. d
2. d
3. a
4. c
5. b
6. c
7. d

Time Period 2 (1775-1800)

Chapter 1
1. d
2. c
3. d
4. c
5. a
6. d

Chapter 2
1. d
2. c
3. c
4. b
5. a

Chapter 3
1. d
2. a
3. d
4. c
5. b

Chapter 4
1. d
2. a
3. b
4. b
5. a

Chapter 5
1. b
2. d
3. d
4. d
5. c
6. c
7. d
8. a

Chapter 6
1. d
2. c
3. a
4. b
5. d
6. d
7. a

Chapter 7
1. d
2. a
3. c
4. d
5. c
6. b

Time Period 3 (1801-1865)

Chapter 1
1. d
2. a
3. a
4. a
5. c
6. a
7. a
8. d
9. c
10. a
11. a

Chapter 2
1. d
2. c
3. a
4. d
5. a
6. c
7. d
8. a
9. a

Chapter 3
1. d
2. b
3. a
4. b
5. c
6. d
7. a

Chapter 4
1. c
2. b
3. b
4. b
5. a
6. d
7. b

Chapter 5
1. c
2. c
3. a
4. d
5. c
6. d
7. a
8. d

Chapter 6
1. d
2. d
3. d

Time period 4 (1866-1900)

Chapter 1
1. d
2. a
3. d
4. c
5. d
6. c
7. c

Chapter 2
1. c
2. d
3. d
4. a
5. d
6. d

Chapter 3
1. d
2. b
3. d
4. b
5. a
6. a
7. a

Chapter 4
1. a
2. c
3. c
4. c
5. b
6. a
7. d
8. b

Chapter 5
1. d
2. d
3. a
4. b
5. a
6. d
7. d

Chapter 6
1. d
2. d
3. d
4. b
5. c
6. a
7. c

Time Period 5 – (1901-1976)

Chapter 1
1. d
2. b
3. d
4. d
5. b
6. a

Chapter 2
1. c
2. c
3. d
4. d
5. b
6. a
7. a
8. c

Chapter 3
1. d
2. a
3. d
4. c
5. a
6. b
7. c
8. a

Chapter 4
1. d
2. d
3. a
4. b
5. c
6. a

Chapter 5
1. a
2. b
3. c
4. d
5. d
6. d
7. d
8. c
9. c

Chapter 6
1. c
2. d
3. d
4. d
5. a
6. b

Chapter 7
1. b
2. d
3. a
4. d
5. d
6. d
7. c

Time Period 6 (1977-2019)
Chapter 1
1. d
2. d
3. b
4. b
5. d
6. a

Chapter 2
1. d
2. d
3. a
4. d
5. a
6. c
7. d

Chapter 3
1. d
2. c
3. b
4. d
5. c
6. a

Chapter 4
1. a
2. b
3. d
4. c
5. d
6. b

Chapter 5
1. d
2. d
3. c
4. a
5. d
6. c
7. a
8. d

Chapter 6
1. d
2. d
3. c
4. a
5. d

Chapter 7
1. b
2. a
3. b
4. a
5. d
6. d
7. d
8. a

REVIEWS

KATHRYN KNIGHT – AUTHOR, AWARD WINNING AFRICAN AMERICAN HISTORIAN

I have truly enjoyed reading "The UntoldStories". For many years the truth has been buried and false narratives about African American history have prevailed, until now. It's thrilling to see your passion to communicate a perspective to our children that isn't currently taught in schools. I would certainly recommend ALL Students across America read it to understand the true history.

GEORGE W. MARTIN - CHAIRMAN OF THE BOARD OF THE URBAN LEAGUE OF MORRIS COUNTY

Yvette takes the reader on an epic journey through Black History. Young and old will be engaged and embark on a journey of self-discovery with surprising results. I think it will spark all readers to want to know more. It is an easy read and a snapshot into our past and present providing an honest and insightful look at our history. I found her fluid prose and questions insightful and thought provoking challenging me to discover more.

JAMES HARRIS, PAST PRESIDENT NEW JERSEY NAACP STATE CONFERENCE, DEAN OF STUDENTS MONTCLAIR UNIVERSITY, CHAIR NEW JERSEY BLACK EDUCATORS

I have read and reviewed African American History: The Untold Story and I endorse it because it provides an excellent primer for educators as well as students.

It is an important contribution to scholarship surrounding African American History and provides concise highlights of important events in the Americas over the centuries since the arrival of enslaved from Africa.

Teachers and students can learn basic facts of American history so they can understand the foundation of current conditions that exist in the United States of America. The extensive list of references affords great opportunities for pursue additional studies in African American history.

BRIAN SHAW – PARENT OF COLLEGE AGED SON AND MIDDLE SCHOOL AGED DAUGHTER

Ms. Long's historical stories will resonate loudly in both the African American Communities and educational community. It is a treat for lovers of history and provides a new perspective on Black History with key questions at the end of each chapter.

This is work of love and an educational journey for many readers. I found myself fascinated and loving this work. She provides an exciting romp through the varied and sometimes surreal landscape of American and African American history. A well-researched journey that many of us have heard whispers of but never saw. She brings the truth to us all about what we contributed.

KEYWORDS

African American

Achievement and black boys

Self-esteem and black boys

Identity

Racial socialization

Black culture

White supremacy

Racism

Misconceptions

Prejudice

Discrimination

Empowerment

Black

White

History

Stories

Africans

ABOUT THE AUTHOR

Yvette Long is the Founder and Executive Director of Platinum Minds, a 501(c)3 not-for-profit organization focused on working with boys and young men from challenged communities. The organization, founded in 2009, provides educational and leadership development skills to boys in sixth through twelfth grades. Platinum Minds also has a reading and mentoring component for younger boys in kindergarten to fifth grades.

As part of the educational and leadership component, the older boys are provided support to stay on a high academic track and to develop leadership skills, community consciousness, and entrepreneurial skills to help foster self-confidence and self-esteem. Yvette's twelve years of experience working with boys and young men have taught her a deeper understanding of what motivates, inspires, and also disenfranchises young men from excelling to their fullest potential.

Yvette holds certifications in counseling and teaching. She holds additional certifications to teach psychology and meditation. She holds a Bachelor of Arts degree in Sociology and Psychology from Thomas Edison State College and a Master's degree in Student Guidance Services from Montclair State University.

Yvette is passionate about the issues preventing individuals from achieving their true potential in life. She has spent a great deal of time volunteering for various organizations as her way of helping to ensure that those with the desire for a better life have the opportunity to realize their dreams. Yvette is the proud recipient of a number of awards, including the Boy Scouts of America Tribute to Women Award (recognized for excellence in working with boys), the Model Citizen Award for New Jersey, and the Outstanding Professional Counselor award from Montclair State University. Yvette lives in Morris County with her husband and their two daughters.

Yvette is also the Founder of Aspire, a counseling and life coaching service aimed at helping young men and individuals acquire the self-esteem and self-awareness they need to be successful on personal and professional levels.

This is her second book, following her earlier one titled "Aspire to Excellence: "Helping Young Men Make Better Choices," available on Amazon.com.

www.africanamericanuts.com

Made in the USA
Middletown, DE
22 June 2020